# kamera
## B O O K S

www.kamerabooks.co.uk

D K Holm

# INDEPENDENT CINEMA

kamera
BOOKS

First published in 2008 by Kamera Books
PO Box 394, Harpenden, Herts, AL5 1XJ
www.kamerabooks.com

Copyright © D K Holm, 2008
Series Editor: Hannah Patterson

A CIP catalogue record for this book is available from the British Library.

ISBN-10: 1-904048-70-6
ISBN-13: 978-1-904048-70-1

Typeset by Avocet Typeset, Chilton, Aylesbury, Bucks
Printed by SNP Lefung Printers (Shenzen) Co Ltd, China

# ACKNOWLEDGEMENTS

I wish to salute numerous friends and colleagues who gave aid during this project, starting with Chris Ryall, former editor of Kevin Smith's website, MoviePoopShoot.com (now QuickStopEntertainment.com), and including Kristi Turnquist of the *Oregonian*, writer Tim Appelo, Holly Cundiff, Helaine Garren, Shawn Levy of the *Oregonian*, filmmakers Patti Lewis and Cynthia Lopez, Andrea Marsden, Cindy Mason, Gregg Morris, L Ninos Smith, Britta Gordon, Mike Russell, Mark Christensen, James Walling, editor of the *Vancouver Voice*, and Charles Schwenk. A large debt is owed to Desiree French, who edited early versions of the text, as well as to the filmmakers who took the time to engage in interviews. More generally, I can cite the Multnomah County Library, the Portland State University Library, and the Internet Movie Database, both Pro and civilian. Acknowledgement is also due to publisher Ion Mills for his enthusiasm and risk-taking, and editor Hannah Patterson for supreme patience.

# CONTENTS

# INTRODUCTION

*'A* picture *held us captive. And we could not get outside it, for it lay in our language and language seemed to repeat it to us inexorably.'*

Ludwig Wittgenstein,
*Philosophical Investigations,*
translator, GEM Anscombe, 1935; Oxford, 1997, No. 115

On 26 June, 1997, George Lucas stepped onto the set of his latest film, *Star Wars Episode I: The Phantom Menace* for its first day of filming. After three years of preparation, consisting of scriptwriting, computer previsualisation, and the assembly of a special effects team and digital camera crew, he was finally ready to commence shooting (though perhaps recording would be a better term) the latest chapter of his ongoing space opera saga. Shot in England, Tunisia and Australia, *Phantom Menace* cost an estimated $115 million to make, all of the money raised by Lucas himself.

Some years later, in May of 2006, a user named Lonelygirl15 began posting her video diary on the website YouTube.com. Named Bree, she was a home-schooled teen who was experiencing new roiling emotions under the influence of the outside world. Her films captured her in activities that ranged from rating different cookie brands to exploring a friendship with 'Daniel', an older boy. In her videotaped, emotional peregrinations, Lonelygirl15 was adding video imagery to a fund of movies that already amounted to over one million posts since YouTube.com first started. Founded in February of 2005 by three former employees of PayPal, a controversial online banking system that has inspired the birth of websites decrying it, YouTube quickly became one of the most visited locations on the Internet, premised on its being a public forum for amateur videos, news clips, music videos, pornography, television commercials and rare TV footage.

Lonelygirl15's posting came at a time when YouTube was proclaiming to enjoy visitations from over 100 million clip-viewers every day, ready to view the 65,000 new video clips that were added daily. Lonelygirl15 proved to be just one of thousands of people who posted their own video blogs. She brought realisation to Francis Ford Coppola's comment about the advances in moviemaking technology – as captured in Fax Bahr and George Hickenlooper's 1991 documentary, *Hearts of Darkness* (about the making of *Apocalypse Now*):

To me, the great hope is that now [sic] these little 8 millimeter video recorders and stuff are coming out some people who normally wouldn't make movies are gonna be making them and suddenly one day some little fat girl in Ohio is going to be the new Mozart and make a beautiful film with her father's little camera recorder and for once the so called 'professionalism' about movies will be destroyed, forever, you know, and it will become an art form.

Lonelygirl15, however, turned out to be a hoax, or more generously, an experiment by a pair of filmmakers, Miles Beckett and Greg Goodfried, who were attempting to generate interest in their work. Bree turned out to be the actress Jessica Lee Rose (among whose films was the Lindsay Lohan vehicle *I Know Who Killed Me*). But still, her movies did what most filmmakers hope their work will: they sparked viewing and commentary. The show and its creators were already represented by the agency CAA. Yet despite the revelation of the show's fictional basis, the resultant solo website, LG15.com, made its debut in the summer of 2006, garnering 150,000 viewers a month there and 300,000 a month on YouTube, where it is still posted.

These filmmakers from extreme ends of the filmmaking spectrum have one thing in common. Both *Star Wars Episode I: The Phantom Menace* and the works of Lonelygirl15 are independent films. One could go so far as to say that they are true independent films, more so than the rash of indie films that preoccupied critical discussion throughout the 1990s, most of which were financed by film studios or distributors of one level of power or another. Seen from the perspective of the work of both George Lucas at one end, and of Lonelygirl15's Beckett and Goodfried, as mentioned above, independent cinema is something of a myth, a bogus term, a false genre.

Almost every book or article or review about independent cinema begins with the author grappling with definitions. Typical is a review of writer-director Rian Johnson's *Brick* in *The Economist* (of 20 May 2006) which begins, 'Defining "independent films" is not easy. Small films? Films that premiere at Robert Redford's Sundance Festival? Films made outside the studio system?'

These are all good answers, posing as questions. What is independent cinema? Is it a school of filmmaking, or is it really simply an economic category, a marketing tool? Can filmmakers ever be truly independent within the context of commercial cinema? And, however it began, hasn't independent cinema by now developed its own style, evolved into a distinct genre?

The reader of *The Economist* suddenly realises that this seemingly simple word 'independent' proves to be as illusive or allusive as the many other words that we take for granted, which, as we start to unravel them, prove complex; words such as 'yet', 'free' and 'reality'. And it is clear that over time 'independent' as an adjective used to describe a movie has altered, be it in the context of commercial or critical usage. In fact, how critics, professional filmmakers and moviegoers have used the word 'independent' over the years helps to chart just what an independent film is even as the definition fluctuates with changing models of film production.

The phrase 'independent cinema' as we now mostly use it came into common parlance around 1977, and strictly speaking served as a designation for movies made outside the confines of traditional financing, distributed by companies that were not aligned to the big Hollywood studios. Though the exhibition business itself usually uses the term 'specialty films' for art house or non-Hollywood product, Harvey and Bob Weinstein, then of Miramax, seized on the word 'independent' as a marketing tool.

Among the films released in 1977 was David Lynch's first feature, *Eraserhead*, initially distributed by Libra Films, a company that existed from around 1971–1982, and also released *Cousin, cousine* and *The Atomic Café*. Joining Lynch's film that year was Joan M Silver's parody of life at an underground newspaper, *Between The Lines*, distributed by Midwest Films, a company that existed solely to distribute Silver's work – which amounted to three films, the first of which was *Hester Street* (1975). In addition, there was John Waters's fifth feature film, *Desperate Living*; his first feature, *Mondo Trasho*, had been released in 1969, but he first became widely known for *Pink Flamingos*, distributed in 1972 by Saliva Films, which existed long enough to release three of Waters's features. Alan Rudolph's first feature *Welcome To LA* was another 1977 release, which made its debut at the Seattle Film Festival in 1976, produced by Robert Altman's company Lions Gate. Altman sold Lions Gate in 1981 and it has since evolved into the most successful non-American film production and distribution company (it is based in Vancouver, BC).

By contrast, here's what the mainstream studios released in 1977: Fox opened *Star Wars*, which made $202 million, Universal offered up *Smokey and the Bandit*, which made $126 million, Columbia released *Close Encounters of the Third Kind*, which made $116 million, Paramount distributed *Saturday Night Fever*, which made $94 million and a movie star of TV actor John Travolta. In addition, MGM released Neil Simon's love comedy *The Goodbye Girl*, which made $41 million. One could argue, though, that *Star Wars* was, in essence, also an independent film, because director George Lucas financed it himself and sold only the distribution rights to Fox, as he would with all subsequent sequels in the series. An analogous person from the world of genre film is George A Romero, a commercial filmmaker who in 1968 formed a small company with a group of friends to film a horror movie outside Pittsburgh called *Night of the Living Dead*. It went on to become not only a big commercial success but one of the most significant influences on pop culture.

The box office for 1977's independent films, on the other hand, is unknown or at least unofficial, but the budget for *Eraserhead* was $100,000, and *Desperate Living* cost $65,000, mere fractions of the financing that went into the majors' releases.

The short-lived small companies that sprang up to distribute these independent directors' films also included, or were soon joined by, larger enterprises such as Circle Releasing, Savoy, Phaedra, October, Gramercy, Trimark, Island, Alive, Live, Goldwyn, Avenue, Vestron, Artisan, Strand, Cannon, New Line, Fine Line and Miramax. All were founded on the principle that audiences had an appetite for non-conformist films stripped of the predictable or familiar story structures of Hollywood cinema, and dealt with issues or political and social concerns ignored by the

studios. At the same time, however, many of these companies conducted themselves like mirror images of their
studio antecedents, wheeling and dealing to outbid each
other for 'product' at film festivals and movie markets, and
merging with each other, or simply failing into disappear-
ance. An amusing insider's look at how independent films
are made is Tom DiCillo's *Living in Oblivion* (1995).

A thumbnail sketch of the history of October Films
summarises the volatile nature of independent film distribution companies from the 1970s on. Bingham Ray, then
an executive unhappy at Avenue Pictures, and Jeff Lipsky,
an executive frustrated at Skouras Pictures, founded
October Pictures in 1991 (taking the name of the company
from Sergei Eisenstein's film, according to Peter Biskind's
*Easy Riders, Raging Bulls*). Their initial desire was to
distribute *Life is Sweet*, British director Mike Leigh's
kitchen sink account of life under Margaret Thatcher.
October subsequently went on to distribute a wide range of
European films (*The Cement Garden*, *Cemetery Man*),
documentaries (*The War Room*), and American indie titles
(*Ruby in Paradise*, *The Last Seduction*). In 1997, Universal
Pictures bought a controlling interest in the company, then
sold its shares to media entrepreneur Barry Diller, who
merged it with Gramercy Pictures (in existence since 1992)
and renamed the resultant whole USA Pictures.
Meanwhile, Universal itself passed through ownership by
Seagrams, Vivendi, before finally ending up in the hands of
NBC. In 2002, Vivendi acquired USA, merged it with
another acquisition, Good Machine, and re-dubbed the
result Focus Features, which, as of the time of writing, is

the art film arm of NBC-Universal's Universal Pictures.

October was only one of several small distribution firms designed to ferry low-budget or specialty films into theatres but that quickly evolved into or were replaced by complex corporations that were independent in name only. Others from the late 1970s onwards have simply disappeared. In such an unstable or protean commercial world, definitions end up transitory, provisional, quickly co-opted.

Yet 'independence' under one label or another has existed within or on the fringes of commercial moviemaking since its inception. The very first films were independent, in their own unique way, because movie studios as we know them didn't exist until the early teens. Since then the sort of film that we now gather under the sole rubric independent was called at various times experimental, underground or avant garde. Other terms include specialty films, art films and fringe filmmaking. One could also argue that foreign films were for a time the contemporaneous equivalent of independent cinema. *Film maudit*, or cursed or disreputable film, is another less used designation, but appropriate for the early films of John Waters and David Lynch. And, arguably, drive-in pictures, grindhouse films, and even stag films and other pornographic works can contain elements or go by standards that affiliate them, to varying degrees, with what we now call independent cinema. America's long history of exploitation films gave birth to the career of African-American director Oscar Micheaux, who financed and physically distributed his films himself. He is the predecessor not only of Spike Lee, whose first movies were student films or independently made, such as *She's Gotta Have It* (1986), but also Melvin Van Peebles (*Sweet Sweetback's Baadasssss Song* [1971]), and Charles Burnett (*Killer of Sheep* [1977]).

In reaching for a definition of independent cinema, it helps to understand what so-called independent cinema is, or believes it is, independent of. In a word, that would be Hollywood. But behind that word is a world of complex interconnections, hierarchies and stages of transition in advancing both a work of art and a commercial property. Hollywood is both a literal place and a state of mind; a factory and a philosophy.

The thumbnail history of Hollywood is simple. Once motion picture production technology was invented in the United States and Europe, it was almost immediately put to commercial use. Kinetoscopes, which required single viewers, were soon replaced by movie theatres, which could accommodate multiple viewers and were more in line with the live theatrical presentations that people were used to, particularly as cinema dropped documentary recordings of reality in favour of fiction. In the first few years of the cinema, Thomas Edison's cameras were leased to groups of filmmakers who struck deals for their product with national exhibitors. By the end of the teens, these disparate groups had formed into stable narrative fiction-making enterprises. The enormous cost of movie producing made the application of the assembly line attractive to investors. This, coupled with the fact that moviemakers were settling in the (then) relatively remote Hollywood, made it feasible for diverse visionaries to establish film studios, where films could be manufactured to the public taste. As movies became a national mania through the 1920s and 1930s, the seven studios – MGM, Fox, Paramount, Warner, Columbia, RKO, Universal – consolidated the very power to make movies amongst themselves. Large Mitchell cameras and 35mm film were prohibitively expensive to other filmmakers who might want to break in.

Speaking broadly, in its early days the filmmakers and the exhibitors 'owned' the movie industry; but with the rise in the medium's popularity came the creation of studios for movie mass production and control of cinema fell into the hands of banks and corporations. By the end of the 1920s, the movie industry was run by a small number of studios, themselves owned or controlled by corporations or banks on the east coast.

In their 'golden age', from the 1930s through the early 1950s, the significant studios were like large theatrical companies. They trained performers and technicians, provided costumes and sets, processed the physical films, advertised them and showed them in their own theatre chains. 'Talent' was hired, trained, exploited, and rose to fame based on a combination of physical appeal, studio mandated publicity, and background networking of all varieties. Movies essentially served the stars, enhancing their images, while at the same time, particularly after the implementation of the Hays office guidelines for tasteful presentation in the early 1930s, shrinking from troublesome realities. Soon there was a national dichotomy between the real world and the 'dream factory'. Filmmakers bristled under the factory's restraints, but went along with them, occasionally pushing the boundaries toward more frankness and political realism.

An exception to this system were the so-called Poverty Row movie studios that included Monogram and Republic. The experiences of directors such as Nicholas Ray, Orson Welles, or Edgar G Ulmer in these studios, as well as those of later directors who worked for companies such as American International, which specialised in drive-in movies, mirrored that of filmmakers in the indie studios of the 1980s and 1990s. They had some freedom as long as they supplied certain components of marketable content. But even in these impoverished studios, conflicts still existed between money and artistic vision. Studio interference existed, just as it did in the majors. Creative ideas were often compromised for big financial returns.

The role of independent cinema in today's popular imagination is that of the rebel child against this corporate 'adult' world of assembly-line filmmaking. If the studios are often less cookie-cutter-like in their approach to filmmaking than critics claim, the so-called independent film is often less 'independent' than it appears to be. To offer a movie that is wholly financed by the Disney Corporation, as most Miramax movies were from 1995 on, and label it 'independent' is simply ludicrous. In both the past and present, changes in the movie industry have come not from within, but via threats from without: competition from foreign films, vast changes in public taste, and severe governmental challenges to studio locks on production and exhibition.

Numerous factors, such as the separation of the studios

from ownership of theatres, labour relations and the advent of commercial television, led to the declining power of the movie studios after the end of World War Two. Producers formerly associated with studios broke away to go it alone, though still remaining tied to the studios via development deals, or 'first-look' options, whereby the studio gets first refusal of a producer's new fare. By the 1960s the movie studios, as creators of film, were moribund. Henceforth, the big seven would be primarily distributors of other people's movies, while the studios themselves were gobbled up by large conglomerates (Paramount by Gulf and Western for a time, though it's currently owned by Viacom). This change didn't necessarily make it easier for outsiders to break into moviemaking, however.

Periodically, Hollywood allows outsiders into the fold in an effort to revitalise itself, like a vampire seeking new victims. One such epoch was that of the late 1960s and early 1970s, traditionally referred to simply as Seventies films. Movies associated with this movement include *Easy Rider*, *Five Easy Pieces*, *Chinatown*, *Carnal Knowledge*, *Coming Home*, and scores of others. During this era, new talents were allowed to express themselves.

Today, film fans talk about how much they love American cinema of the 1970s but when modern filmmakers pay homage to the films of their youth no one goes to see them. Three recent such examples were the films *Zodiac*, *Breach*, and *The Good Shepherd*. All three are expensive, well-mounted, serious, moody films about real events, and each adopts different aspects of 1970s films as colours on its palette. *Breach*'s look and feel has its roots in *All the*

*President's Men*, *The Good Shepherd* evokes *The Godfather Part II*, and *Zodiac* draws on numerous 70s films set in San Francisco, such as *Dirty Harry*, for its look, particularly in its interiors.

All these films 'flopped' at the box office, perhaps because word of mouth suggested they were slow and anti-dramatic. But then most of the films from the seventies that are now heralded as masterpieces were also flops. And many of them tended to be measured and static. *The Paper Chase*, for example, one of the few indie-style hits of the time, is surprisingly slow paced, ponderous and oblique in its storytelling, additionally hampered by passages of shallow, out-of-date humour.

Soon enough, however, movies were popular again and the invitations to outsiders dried up. Throughout the 1980s, the movie studios, *mutatis mutandis*, conducted themselves much as they did in the 1930s, though arguably with even less soul. Now, what the studios do is create or co-opt franchises with brands, such as X-men, Batman and Indiana Jones. In response, what the so-called independent studios do, with the exception of Miramax's division Dimension and New Line, is create a brand with a director, Quentin Tarantino, say, or Ang Lee.

Each era's fringe filmmaking gets the label it deserves. It also gets the filmmakers it deserves. Economic conditions fluctuate and prevailing cultural trends may wither the ambitions of some, while others overcome difficulties to create works that seem diametrically opposed to the current trend of filmmaking.

The rise of independent film mirrors advances in light-weight and inexpensive filmmaking technology. Kodak introduced 16mm film in 1923 and gradually its utility for newsreels and documentary, and later television, made it popular in the industry, but Kodak intended it for use by the amateur market. Home use of film didn't really take off until the introduction of much more accessible 8mm film, originally made available in 1932 but reaching its peak of popularity from the late 1950s onward. However, artists and aspiring filmmakers took advantage of the 16mm format to dabble in cinema, so Maya Deren, for example, could make a film such as *Meshes of the Afternoon*, just one of many 'non-film' people who were able now to encroach on the art of cinema.

An early example of an 'independent' film is *The Life and Death of 9413, a Hollywood Extra*; a movie about the movies, it uses the world of filmmaking as the basis and setting for a tale of existential absurdity. Written by Robert Florey and Slavko Vorkapich, and directed by and starring Florey, the film is about one Raucourt (played by Jules Raucourt), aka 9413. He has come to Hollywood dreaming of fame, but ends up at the bottom of the cinematic food chain with a number on his head; in a phantasmagoric ending he ascends to heaven, where the number is finally removed. Shot by cinematographer Gregg Toland, who went on to film *Citizen Kane*, at 11 minutes it was categorised simply as a short film, but in spirit it attempts to shed the imperialism of Hollywood, criticising or shunning its closed system of values, possibilities, and narrative strategies, already apparent by the 1920s, and instead say

something 'true' about social interaction and human potential.

Florey had already directed several feature films (*The
Romantic Age* [1927]; *Hello New York* [1928]) by the time
he made this short, but as a French man out of his own
country it's possible he felt an empathy with Raucourt's
plight and existential crisis. He ended up as one of a league
of filmmakers generally referred to, and not without a
measure of admiration, as Hollywood professionals, toiling
on little-remembered titles. After *The Life and Death of
9413*, Vorkapich went on to have a modest if long career in
Hollywood, primarily as an editor and special effects tech-
nician, though he did direct around ten films. He died in
Spain in 1976, three years before Florey.

Another Hollywood professional who flirted with 'independence' as we perhaps know it today was Texas-born
director King Vidor (1894–1982). In 1934, he released *Our
Daily Bread*. Spurned by the studios, Vidor financed the film
himself, eventually getting a $125,000 bank loan with his
house as collateral, bitterly paradoxical given that the
banking system receives a lot of criticism in the script. *Our
Daily Bread* recounts the trials and tribulations of a young
couple (Tom Keene, Karen Morley) who idealistically work a
tough spit of land with an accumulated co-operative of
eccentrics. The story ends with a thrilling sequence in
which the collective attempts to build an irrigation ditch in a
race against time. The editing of this sequence is very
much in the spirit of Soviet films of the era, and the film
received a certificate of merit at the 1935 Soviet
International Exposition of Film. The ambiguity of this

embrace is probably rooted in the film's own ambiguity, neither fully left nor right, populist nor egalitarian, and it was released in America by United Artists at a time when, given the economic climate, stories about working people were surprisingly sparse on the screen. Suffice to say, Vidor's example was not followed, by Vidor himself or anyone else for some time.

Meanwhile, in Europe, French playwright Marcel Pagnol (1895–1974) turned to filmmaking in 1933, essentially giving up the theatre, a controversial move at the time, given his new-found prestige. Films such as *Merluse* (1935), *Topaze* (1936) and *Cesar* (1936), all based on his own plays, proved equally popular with the public. Later films such as *The Baker's Wife* (1938) were set in the rural peasant environment that he favoured, and often based on adaptations from the work of Jean Giono, who specialised in such milieux. More recently, the 1986 art house hits *Jean de Florette* and *Manon of the Spring* have been adapted from his novels. European film financing worked completely differently from the American model, and Pagnol created his own production company, Les Auteurs Associes. Financed by and then staffed with relatives, the company proved successful. He ceased making films in the mid-1950s, just as his early work was being reevaluated by critics such as Andre Bazin, whose arguments in defence of his films helped elevate Pagnol's body of work; and it served as one of many inspirations for the French New Wave.

In the United States filmmaking equipment was slowly becoming more accessible to the public. In response, 'amateurs' from all walks of life began to try their hand at the art form. Among them were Maya Deren (1917–1961), a woman on the fringes of the New York art scene of the 1940s, and her husband Alexander Hammid, a photographer. They collaborated on *Meshes of the Afternoon* (1943), a sardonic, heavily 'Freudian' and symbolic film – though the symbolism appears to derive entirely from a private lexicon – that looms large in film history for the inspiration it generated.

Meanwhile, in Southern California, people who grew up on the fringes of Hollywood acquired lightweight cameras, gathered friends, and made 'weekend' short films. Kenneth Anger (born in 1927) made the gay-themed *Fireworks* (1947) in his parents' house while they were on a trip. His then-friend Curtis Harrington (1926–2007) directed and starred in *Fragment of Seeking* (1946) and *Picnic* (1948). Eventually Harrington entered the film business proper, making a series of campy horror films with interrogative titles such as *Whoever Slew Auntie Roo?* and *What's the Matter with Helen?* Anger stayed on the outside, making increasingly ornate and private short films while also compiling the gossip books *Hollywood Babylon* and *Hollywood Babylon II*. Anger and Harrington, as well as later underground filmmakers such as George Kuchar and Jack Smith, found moviemaking to be an alternative environment in which they could explore their sexuality and the underground culture at the time. In this regard, underground films of the 1940s through to the early 1970s were true independent films: independent of corporate financing but also independent of prevailing social dictates or prejudices.

In the American film business, the studios traditionally control financing, exhibition and, most importantly, distribution are dealt with by different but aligned companies. Therefore, throughout most of film history, it has been difficult to make a 'major motion picture' outside that system. A filmmaker might manage to gather enough money to rent the equipment to shoot the film, but once it's completed, how can he or she find a way of showing it to people? *Salt of the Earth* (1954), like *Our Daily Bread*, was a rare exception. Directed by Herbert J Biberman, and written by Biberman with Michael Wilson, the film told the story of the Grant County, New Mexico, miners' strike, which occurred only a few years before Biberman made the film. It chronicles the difficulties that Mexican-American mine workers faced when they struck for wages equal to those of their Anglo-American co-workers (among other issues) and shows the resolve of the miners' wives when they take up the cause themselves at the end.

*Salt of the Earth* was produced entirely outside the Hollywood system, and thanks to its subject matter, which included labour and union matters, race relations and the feminist movement, the United States government and the media harassed the production and the film itself. The film was pro-labour and pro-union, and partially financed by the International Union of Mine, Mill and Smelter Workers, believed to be a mostly communist-affiliated leadership. Media response to the film was mostly harsh. Reviewer Pauline Kael gave the film one of its most negative reviews, writing in *Sight and Sound* in 1954 that *Salt of the Earth* was 'as clear a piece of Communist propaganda as we have had in many years'.

Director Biberman was a member of the group who came to be known as the Hollywood Ten, who, when called to testify about their supposed communist leanings, served six months in prison for refusing to co-operate with the body set up for that investigation, the House Un-American Activities Committee. Afterwards, he lived mostly in European exile.

Influenced by a mix of Pagnol, Roberto Rossellini and the Neo-realists, and also film criticism, the French New Wave in its turn influenced Hollywood cinema during the time that new talents were gaining a footing. The New Wave stood in opposition to what the movement's in-house newsletter, *Cahiers du cinema*, called the 'tradition of quality', which makes the New Wave independent cinema at least in spirit. What directors such as Jean-Luc Godard, Francois Truffaut, Claude Chabrol, Jacques Rivette and Eric Rohmer seemed to share was a liberating feeling that they could do anything, whether it be shoot on the street, make political statements, or knowingly mimic and quote their favourite Hollywood films. The business model of European film production is different from the US system and will be discussed in more detail later but in general suffice to say it's more receptive to dissenting views and serious subject matter.

Through biographies of film stars, writers and directors, a reader quickly learns that many of the members of the studio system were frustrated with its anodyne product and restrictive subject matter, especially actors who came out of the theatre and studied new approaches to the form such as Method acting. John Cassavetes (1929–1989) is a good example of a truly independent filmmaker who emerged in frustration from the studio system to go against the grain of mainstream filmmaking ideas. Like Orson Welles, much of his screen acting after the early 1960s was for the purpose of raising money to fund his own string of 13 remarkable films, including *Faces* (1968), *Husbands* (1970), and *A Woman Under the Influence* (1974), most of them financed and distributed independently of the studios. He also served as a role model and hero for younger directors including Martin Scorsese and Abel Ferrara.

Not all actors-turned-directors are so ambitious or successful. For every heir to Cassavetes's passion, such as Sean Penn, there are several who don't take to the job, such as Tom Hanks, or Bill Murray, who co-directed a brilliant comedy, *Quick Change* (1990), but subsequently stopped directing. Some, however, keep trying. Edward Burns, for instance, alternates between acting and making indie films. And then there's Vincent Gallo. A fashion model, painter, musician and actor, Gallo shot his first feature film, *Buffalo '66*, independently in 1998 for $1.5 million. Though uneven in tone, the film went on to win a Best First Feature Award at the Independent Spirit Awards.

His second feature came five years later, the controversial *The Brown Bunny* (2003). Gallo made these films on his own, defiant in the face of industry indifference, but he was also savvy enough to know that his wicked persona (he put a curse on film critic Roger Ebert for panning *Brown Bunny*) was perfect to generate free publicity in newspapers and magazines. Despite the technical filmmaking burdens he put on himself, Gallo seemed to relish directing. On a side note, Gallo's barbed cinematic aggressiveness plays in stark contrast to the sweet-tempered work of fellow (non-acting) indie filmmakers such as Nicole Holofcener (*Walking and Talking*, 1996), or Kimberly Pierce, whose *Boys Don't Cry* (1999) courted controversy.

While Cassavetes was beginning to explore the possibilities of independent feature films, the 1960s also enjoyed the rise of the underground film, and its wide variety of practitioners including Andy Warhol (*Chelsea Girls* [1966]), Stan Brakhage (*Dog Star Man* [1962]), Jordan Belson (*Phenomena* [1968]), Bruce Conner (*Marilyn Times Five* [1973]), and Michael Snow (*Wavelength* [1967]). These works were often, beneath their crazy surface, autobiographical, or experimental, as they were often referred to: experiments in filmic technique and technology to see what the medium could bear. These films circulated utterly outside the commercial film world, generally via small 16mm distribution companies or with the artists themselves taking them on lecture-workshop tours.

Another important branch of independent film is the documentary. A much sought-after option by viewers who are bored with traditional Hollywood fare, the documentary feature really started to take off in the late 1980s. The success of films by Michael Moore (*Roger & Me* [1989], *Bowling for Columbine* [2002], *Fahrenheit 9/11* [2004], *Sicko* [2007]), Errol Morris (*Gates of Heaven* [1980], *The Thin Blue Line* [1988]), and Ross McElwee (*Sherman's March: A Mediation to the Possibility of Romantic Love in the South During an Era of Nuclear Weapons Proliferation* [1986] and *Bright Leaves* [2003]) were all on a par with modest fiction feature films. All stretched the definition of documentary in interesting ways, through reconstructed scenes, a wide streak of humour, or deeply personal auto-biographical accounts.

In recent years, dot com millionaires have financed their own films. Moviefone founder Andrew Jarecki went on to make *Capturing the Friedmans* (2003), about how charges of paedophilia against a father and son affects a Long island, New York family, and software entrepreneur Charles Ferguson sold his product FrontPage to Microsoft and later went on to make *No End in Sight* (2007), a detailed exami-nation of the executive decisions that led to the American quagmire in Iraq.

As important as the filmmakers who made underground or experimental films were the book writers, curators and independent exhibitors who gave them what meagre publicity they received. Among their most consistent supporters was Amos Vogel, who founded Cinema 16 in New York City, a pioneering institution that screened the films of Deren, Anger and Conner, amongst others, as well as the feature films of John Cassavetes and the French New Wave. He also co-founded the New York Film Festival. Vogel is the author of the book *Film as a Subversive Art*, and both this book and other facets of his career are portrayed in the documentary that accompanies this book.

One of the most remarkably tenacious careers in all independent cinema is that of Jon Jost, who was born in 1943 and began making feature films in 1974. A draft dodger who served a few years in a federal penitentiary, Jost was a radical filmmaker at the height of the radical movement, and his films often show a complete absence of regard for traditional cinematic narrative conventions. Among his most notable works, all self-distributed, are *Last Chants for a Slow Dance* (1977) and *All the Vermeers in New York* (1990).

One of the first filmmakers to whom the label independent was attributed was the late Eagle Pennell (1952–2002), the Texas-based director of *The Whole Shootin' Match* (1978) and *Last Night at the Alamo* (1983). Pennell was part of a surprisingly active film community, and in his life and work anticipated the Austin film community, represented by Richard Linklater and Robert Rodriguez, among others. Also in 1978, the same year as *The Whole Shootin' Match*, came *Northern Lights*. Co-directed by John Hanson and Rob Nilsson in Minnesota, this documentary-style film tracks the origins of the now forgotten Nonpartisan League, a farmers' organisation, and evinced the stolidity, seriousness and grimness of early independent feature films.

These films were followed shortly in theatres by Victor Nunez's 1979 film *Gal Young 'Un*, the story, adapted from a novel by Marjorie Kinnan Rawlings, of a woman who confronts her husband's much younger mistress. Costing only $40,000, *Gal Young 'Un* was financed in part by the National Endowment for the Arts, which was granting money to moviemakers at the time, by the Chubb Corporation, an insurance conglomerate, and by PBS. Distribution was minimal but the film toured the festival circuit and aired on PBS. Nunez was a true auteur, writing, directing, shooting and editing the film, which he continued to do by and large in his subsequent films, *Ruby in Paradise* (1993) and *Ulee's Gold* (1997). Nunez was also a founding member of the Independent Feature Project, a national organisation that sponsors screenings and workshops and publishes the magazine *Filmmaker*. The organisation may well have helped further the use of the word 'independent' as a discrete type of filmmaking.

Richard Pearce's *Heartland*, also released in 1979 and self-distributed, was consistent with some of the other real, early independent films; a rather grimly realistic tale, in this case about pioneering the West. Pearce went on, however, to lead a conventional Hollywood career.

Though most critics tag the release of Steven Soderbergh's *sex, lies and videotape* in 1989 as the 'birth' of independent cinema as we know it today, in fact the 'movement' was born in 1980 with John Sayles's popular and successful *Return of the Secaucus 7*. Sayles is a novelist turned filmmaker, who won a MacArthur Foundation Grant in 1983, and is also a prolific screenwriter. His films can be uneven and as such are unevenly successful but he has remained fiercely independent and now has a significant 16-film body of work as a director. *Secaucus 7* initiated a turn in the so-called independent film. Like his successors, he eventually aimed for a broader audience, but by embracing contentiously political subjects, rather than personal, non-dramatic tales, historical subjects, or delicate adaptations of short stories.

On 19 June 2007, *Variety*'s Marc Graser reported the

latest news about Lonelygirl15. The creators had signed a deal with the cosmetic company Neutrogena to introduce a new character, a 22-year-old scientist who will help Bree in her adventures. This was nothing new, however. The previous January, the show's creators had incorporated Hershey's Icebreakers Sours gum as a less-than-subliminal ad for the candy. At the same time, the show's producers were on the verge of launching their new show, *KateModern*, on the website Bebo.com, with characters designed to appeal to viewers in the UK, Ireland, Australia and New Zealand. Meanwhile, after *Star Wars Episode I: The Phantom Menace* was released on 19 May 1999, it went on to make $922,379,000.

Thus did the sun set on independent cinema.

And perhaps that is a good thing. What we have come to call 'Independent Cinema' has evolved from experimental works by filmmakers free of corporate supervision to what amounts to a genre unto itself, but a dry, predictable, ener-vated genre, closely stage managed by corporations. Lisa Rosman, in a 11 July 2007 entry on her blog *The Broad View* (http://lisarosman.blogspot.com/), reflects a growing disenchantment with so-called independent cinema. 'Anyone who's read this blog over the last few years knows of my mounting frustration with the American independent film scene,' she writes. 'Why I reserve my ire for this world rather than Hollywood is simple: I refuse to play frog to the scorpion of the major studio system. Complaining that a major motion picture is crap is pretty much like whining that Twinkies don't yield nutritional value.' She goes on to add that, 'If Hollywood reflects America's unchecked capitalist impulse, the state of US indies reflects our enormous identity crisis in its wake.' Rosman concludes that, 'Most indie fare these days suffers from over-earnestness of one ilk or another. There are the Sayles babies, who attempt to solve or at least tackle all the world's problems in one fell swoop. Even those ventures that are banging in theory still go down like medicine that could use a spoonful of sugar. Then there are the many indie filmmakers content to merely approach their own problems via the medium of film. Admittedly, this self-searching, however initially masturbatory, has served as the chief impetus of most art since the beginning of time.'

This book attempts to define, or redefine if you will, independent film, by looking at how the phrase is used in relation to a small cadre of filmmakers labelled as independent. These filmmakers also serve as examples of variants on independent cinema. The career of Jill Sprecher illustrates the difficulties an intellectual and philosopher has in creating motion pictures. James Mangold's career shows how independent cinema, at least in the 1990s, could serve as a springboard to mainstream or commercial cinema. Canadian Guy Maddin is a rarity: a filmmaker who has thus far remained true to his code as a 'primitivist', or 'garage band' filmmaker, shooting his movies in Winnipeg with excruciatingly low budgets and no concern for appeasing mainstream audience expectations. Whit Stillman's films illustrate the patience a filmmaker must have if he is going to remain true to his philosophy and vision, while still making popular entertainment. Each of these filmmakers could bear to have individual volumes written about them (and I am currently working on a book about Maddin), but here the focus is exclusively on their careers as independent filmmakers, with sidelights into their thematic concerns.

# INDEPENDENT CINEMA AS ALTERNATIVE TO COMMERCIAL STORYTELLING: JILL AND KAREN SPRECHER

If you wanted to come up with a style guide to a modern independent film, the first port of call would be the films of Jill and Karen Sprecher. Their films provide a checklist of core indie components. In the sceptical imagination, a typical American independent film is a precious, twee tale notable for its novelty casting of, say, Shelley Winters, or some other semi-retired star from the classical age, opposite, say, Pee-Wee Herman and two or three young adult stars from contemporary sitcoms, all enacting scenes set in one huge, budget-preserving house in which various relatives gather for a contentious Thanksgiving dinner, which results in tears, smiles and hugs. The satire of independent cinema, *For Your Consideration* (2006), got the solo setting and the washed-up actress right, but in other respects Christopher Guest's normally accurate anthropology was defeated by a lack of observed reality; for example, indie films of the type he parodied are almost always set in the present, rather than the American South in the 1940s, and usually on practical location sets rather than in Los Angeles studios.

Films by the Sprechers do indeed have some of these comical components, but with one major difference. Their films are good.

Jill and Karen Sprecher are the Coen Sisters of indie cinema. The Midwest natives make films solely from their original screenplays, which Jill directs and Karen produces, although these traditional divisions of labour blur and interact. Jill Sprecher went to the University of Wisconsin, where she received a degree in philosophy and literature, then moved to New York where she studied film and worked on the periphery of the film industry, as, among other roles, a production coordinator. There are other directors who came to filmmaking from a circuitous route. Horror maestro Wes Craven was an English professor, and in the 1990s there was a vogue for painters turning to filmmaking, with Julian Schnabel helming *Basquiat* (1996) and *Before Night Falls* (2000), and Robert Longo directing *Johnny Mnemonic* (1995). Karen Sprecher, meanwhile, graduated from the University of Wisconsin, and then received an MSW from New York University, after which she worked as a clinical social worker counselling teens and young adults in Chicago. Her 'break' into show business came during a visit to Jill in New York City, when her sister hired her as an assistant production coordinator on an independent film. Karen then went on to work on several indies including *The Last Good Time*, *Stonewall* and *Enemies: A Love Story*.

Jill and Karen began writing *Clockwatchers* together on weekends 'as a diversion', according to Jill, 'never thinking it would get made. That's about it. We're lazy.'

The Sprechers' *Clockwatchers* made its debut at the Sundance Film Festival and won prizes at other international festivals in 1997. It is quintessentially 'indie' in its use of a varied cast, including Lisa Kudrow, then one of the stars of the sitcom *Friends*, Parker Posey, a young actress who was rapidly becoming an axiom of independent cinema, and Toni Collette, a respected Australian actress. It was also confined to one setting, primarily a single floor of a business office. Their subsequent film, *Thirteen Conversations About One Thing*, was a top ten-list film favourite of many critics and viewers in 2001.

Some might detect a little of the early Woody Allen in the Sprechers' films. Just as Allen inserted references to books such as *The Denial of Death* and other serious works into his comedies, the Sprechers are absorbed by large questions of happiness and meaning in life. In both *Clockwatchers* and *Thirteen Conversations*, an unhappy central character performs a selfless gesture that changes, in some small, perhaps even unseen way, the life of another. As Bertrand Russell wrote in *The Conquest of Happiness*, one of Jill Sprecher's favourite books, 'So long as [a person] continues to think about the cause of his unhappiness, he continues to be self-centered and therefore does not get outside the vicious circle... The happy life is to an extraordinary extent the same as the good life.'

But a significant difference between films by the Sprechers and other similar-seeming filmmakers is the milieu in which their characters appear, which is generally the workaday world, complete with its class differences and hierarchies. In this way, the Sprechers resemble the screenwriters and directors of the Warner Bros films of the 1930s and such later gritty filmmakers and writers as Samuel Fuller, Paddy Chayefsky and Richard Brooks (at least in late films such as *Looking for Mr Goodbar*).

Jill Sprecher's untraditional route into the movie business suggests one reason why she favours screenplays with ordinary life content over special-effects-driven tales. She is interested in stories rather than lavish visual pyrotechnics. She wants to explore the truth of human dynamics rather than offer the viewer something to simply pass the time. She therefore shoots her films in a deliberate style with only subtle flourishes, when she draws, for example, on the visual style of a specific painter. Not only does the Sprechers' concentration on working life assure their films entry into the 'independent film' world, but also into a rising genre among indie films.

On the surface *Clockwatchers* seems to be just another arty suspense film, a slim tale of revenge, with one of those existential edges that makes movies seem 'thoughtful'. Or it could be called a stalker film, a favourite genre of young filmmakers trying to break into Hollywood. But in fact it's an addition to a whole new genre, or sub-genre, of the 'workaday' film, which, for want of a better phrase, could be called 'heroic alienation'.

Heroic Alienation films tend to be big productions set in small worlds, and generally follow the travails of a lead character who finds the corporate world dispiriting. There are a surprising number of films in this genre. Among them are Mike Judge's *Office Space* (1999), Richard Linklater's *subUrbia* (1996), Todd Haynes's *Safe* (1995), and most of the films directed by Wes Anderson, PT Anderson, and the sardonic Todd Solondz. There's even a foreign contingent, with Denys Arcand's *Le Déclin de l'empire américain* (1986), Jaco van Dormael's *Toto le Heros* (1991), the late Jean-Claude Lauzon's *Leolo* (1992), and Laurent Cantet's *Time Out* (2001), among many others. Most genre-defining, however, are the Sprechers' *Clockwatchers*, Sam Mendes's *American Beauty* (1999), Neil LaBute's *In the Company of Men* (1997) and *Your Friends and Neighbors* (1998) and David Fincher's *Fight Club* (1999), a mix of independent releases and studio projects. These last films lay the foundation for the alienated worker themes of the genre, where people lead drab lives while oppressed in the workspace, their dreams frustrated, the office politics vicious.

In *American Beauty* and Mark Romanek's *One Hour Photo* (2002) one can discern a more explicitly vicious attack on the American family as an institution that's corrupt to its core, at best a fraud, a 1950s-style charade that squashes the life out of everyone, not only those in it, but also those on the outside, achingly, misguidedly looking in.

The rise of a genre such as Heroic Alienation is unimaginable without the latitude and creative freedom that independent cinema, at its best, offers. Although Billy Wilder's *The Apartment* (1960) is similar to *Clockwatchers* and was made more or less within the traditional Hollywood system, in the present day the increasingly cookie-cutter feel of Hollywood's output from the mid-1980s on has closed off whole areas of the American experience to filmgoers. It probably also helped that most Heroic Alienation films are comedies, making them more palatable to the public. By contrast, network television traffics almost wholly in 'work place' stories, from sitcoms to crime shows. It was a paradox of the 1950s that workers would come home from eight-hour shifts and sit down before television shows that reiterated the experiences they'd just escaped from. But were it not for original filmmakers such as Jill and Karen Sprecher, who felt the urge to explore this facet of American life, there would probably be much less American film worth watching.

### *Clockwatchers* (1997)

**Directed by:** Jill Sprecher
**Written by:** Jill Sprecher, Karen Sprecher
**Produced by:** Gina Resnick
**Edited by:** Stephen Mirrione
**Cinematography:** Jim Denault
**Cast:** Toni Collette (Iris Chapman), Parker Posey (Margaret Burre), Lisa Kudrow (Paula), Alanna Ubach (Jane), Helen FitzGerald (Cleo), Jamie Kennedy (Eddie), Bob Balaban (Milton Lasky), Paul Dooley (Bud Chapman)

*Clockwatchers* is about the experiences of Iris Chapman (Toni Collette), a temp hired by Global Credit, an anonymous and tense working place. There she meets and briefly befriends three other women, all of whom are oppressed by their jobs, and at odds with society. Margaret Burre (Parker Posey) is the crazy, rebellious one; Paula (Lisa

Kudrow) is an aspiring actress; and the life of Jane (Alanna Ubach) revolves around her fiancé. A series of office thefts makes everyone mutually suspicious, and draws scrutiny onto the temp staff, who are eventually corralled in Kafkaesque paranoia. Gradually, the temps leave. Only Iris is left, and she sets out to solve the mystery of the thefts and bring a form of justice to her experience.

*Clockwatchers* has many of the 'features of convenience' of a typical 'independent' movie. The narrative takes place mostly in one place: the office space shared by the temps. Auxiliary locations include the bathroom, coatroom, a smoking area, the street outside their building and a nearby bar. The poverty of location actually works to the film's advantage, suggesting and inducing claustrophobia and constriction. *Clockwatchers* also shows indie spirit in its eclectic selection of cast members. More important, it does not attempt to tell a crime story (though there is a crime at the centre of the plot), a romance or comedy (though it is funny in the satirical spirit of, say, William Gaddis's novel *JR*). Rather it tells an 'eccentric' tale in a setting that's unusual for American movies, the workspace, examining the lives of 'ordinary' women. In effect, we already have the traditional 'Hollywood' version of this story, in the form of the outlandish 1993 thriller *The Temp*.

*Clockwatchers* begins with Iris (Toni Collette) waiting in the foyer of Global Credit Associated. She is a temp arriving for her first day of work, but the receptionist (Joshua Malina, later of series *The West Wing*) is reading a catalogue while waiting for the clock to announce the beginning of his workday. He won't 'do business' until 9 am.

Iris instantly establishes herself as a meek and mousy person (she waits an unnecessary two hours before starting work because she takes literally the instructions someone has given her to 'sit and wait'). The corporation is presented as a spare, impersonal place, with only its name adorning the walls, and with everyone playing strictly by a set of rules passed among the employees like some kind of bureaucratic oral tradition.

The tableau of the opening shot and scene establishes this dichotomy. Iris is a 'have not'; she is a temp, the lowest possible person in a business hierarchy because she isn't really an employee. The pastels of the lobby are consistent throughout Global Credit's work environment; a pathetically cheerful series of colours augmented by non-stop Muzak. Iris is instantly sucked into this inhuman and hierarchical place, one that is at once both impersonal yet competitive. This workspace sits within a cinematic tradition; the Sprechers drew upon King Vidor's *The Crowd* (1928), for example, Ermanno Olmi's *Il Posto* (*The Sound of Trumpets* [1961]) and Wilder's *The Apartment* (which itself nods at *The Crowd* with its uniform mass office space).

Iris soon finds herself swept up into the concerns of the office's three other temps. First she meets Margaret who tells Iris that the woman she is temping for, Louise, won't be back for a while. Margaret shows Iris the lay of the land, pointing out who is fussy, who controls supplies, and who has a shoe fetish. Margaret is the most dynamic of the film's characters, the sort viewers often wish they could be, reckless and perverse, flouting convention. In contrast, Jane and Paula are self-deluding, one about the sanctity of her forthcoming marriage, the second about her talent. Sprecher distinguishes the women from each other subtly, through vocal mannerisms, colours and clothes, even down to the different watches they wear (Iris's falsely peppy Swatch versus Margaret's unconventional man's watch).

Having established the players, Sprecher then introduces the drama. Margaret, for all her rebelliousness, is nevertheless irked when an executive, Mr Lasky, hires a 'much needed' assistant. Because she has been passed over, Margaret announces that she hates the building and everyone in it. The new assistant is Chloe, and she is, if possible, even mousier than Iris. There is an immediate unspoken and complex bond between them, while in contrast the other temps, spearheaded by Margaret, loathe her and conspire against her. When office artifacts begin to disappear, Margaret immediately suspects Chloe, but GCA employees higher up the ladder find Margaret and the temps more likely candidates. Meanwhile, Iris's home life is explained. Her widowed father is a salesman who is upbeat about his daughter's prospective ability in the same profession. He can't see her nervousness and insecurity; yet these aspects of her character gradually change throughout the film as she absorbs the best features of her disappearing friends: rebelliousness in the face of oppression, loyalty to friends, and the performance skills necessary to get by in an office.

Like Lee Holloway (Maggie Gyllenhaal) in *Secretary* (2002),

Iris is taking the job as a temp in order to break out of the slough of despond, unconsciously stage managed by her benevolently cheerleading father. In Margaret, she meets her polar opposite, a woman who scoffs at authority, uses the work place as her private playground, and scorns rules. At the same time, there is still something conventional about Margaret. Her purpose at Global Credit is to get a recommendation, which will help her advance to permanent employment at some other institution. This seems like a sadly circumscribed goal for such a vivacious personality. The variety and subtlety of the characters portrayed in this film are gratifyingly well observed, observed from life.

The complexities and the subtleties of *Clockwatchers* are primarily in design, camera placement and the ironies of the plot's incidents. But there is another crucial element: Iris narrates the film. Narration is a common feature of the independent film, yet it is also a direct violation of the precepts expounded by Robert McKee, say, in his screenwriting manual *Story: Substance, Structure, Style, and the Principles of Screenwriting*. These precepts are themselves ridiculed by example in another quasi-independent film, Spike Jonze and Charlie Kaufman's *Adaptation*. In *Clockwatchers*, the narration is strangely reassuring. The fact that Iris talks to us suggests that she will ultimately turn out all right, thus freeing us to enjoy the rudderless insanity of the office space she is temporarily trapped in.

## *Thirteen Conversations About One Thing* (2001)

**Directed by:** Jill Sprecher
**Written by:** Jill Sprecher, Karen Sprecher
**Produced by:** Gina Resnick, Beni Atoori
**Edited by:** Stephen Mirrione
**Cinematography:** Dick Pope
**Cast:** Clea DuVall (Beatrice), Alan Arkin (Gene), Matthew McConaughey (Troy), John Turturro (Walker), Amy Irving (Patricia), Barbara Sukowa (Helen), Frankie Faison (Richard Lacey), Tia Texada (Dorrie)

As listed in the end credits of *Thirteen Conversations About One Thing,* the Sprechers have divided the film's world and its characters into four subdivisions. There are the Attorneys, led by Troy, who commits a hit and run and then withers into inactive guilt over it; there are the Academics, in which a woman named Patricia loses her physics professor husband Walker, who has been having an affair with a colleague; there are the Housekeepers, primarily Beatrice, the victim of the hit and run, who also has a secret crush on one of her clients, who, rather than return her affection, obliviously and casually accuses her of theft; and finally the Claims Adjusters, in which Gene is the preoccupied head of a typically disgruntled office, who observes the unpredictable up and down luck of those around him. The lives of the characters intersect and overlap, usually without their larger awareness, and the real timeframe of the narrative is withheld until the end.

If Iris is the person who more or less sacrifices herself,

or at least her job, for the good of others in *Clockwatchers*, then Gene is the noble character of *Thirteen Conversations*. He is like the philosopher-philanthropist advocated in the novel *Magnificent Obsession* by Lloyd C Douglas, which was adapted to screen twice. He is also like Iris, but downtrodden by the external world rather than any inner insecurities. Gene invisibly helps others, while he himself is in pain thanks to a divorce and troubles with his drug-addicted son. In addition, Gene has a spectre of authority about him. He runs an office not unlike the one in *Clockwatchers*, be it slightly more human and much more cramped. Bitterness over his lot in life initially hampers his natural efforts toward doing good work.

The Sprechers' second feature film is what writer Shawn Levy calls a 'web of life' movie. Other examples from the same time period as *Thirteen Conversations* include *Playing by Heart* (1998), *Sliding Doors* (1998), and *Me Myself I* (1999). Gene's sacrifices mean little in the small picture, but in the big picture the film's omniscience provides, he changes several lives. As we watch the story unfold, and the silent connections between several of the characters are revealed, the movie communicates a stronger net of connection than the characters themselves can see or express.

*Thirteen Conversations* comes in a narrative shape that one doesn't typically associate with a studio release. It leaps around, backtracks then leaps forward, follows one character and then shifts to another, seemingly haphazardly. The film is also subdivided into units, which are announced with titles that reiterate a snippet of dialogue from that sequence. *Thirteen Conversations* demands concentration. As in Quentin Tarantino's *Reservoir Dogs* (1992) and *Pulp Fiction* (1994), there is great play with the time line. For example, the narrative begins at a particular point, juggles the different tangents of the story, and leaps backwards (though the viewer doesn't know it yet). Everything appears to be happening within the same time period, but then a character mentions that a year has passed; the viewer realises that a scene enacted at the beginning is actually the prelude to one of the subplots, which now will play out beyond the confines of the film's running time.

*Conversations* begins and ends with Patricia looking at the world through a window. The arc of her story in the film begins and ends with those windows. Windows figure highly in the film, as Gene's office has windows that reveal him to his employees and vice versa. Each of the film's four worlds is characterised by a particular look. Patricia's is out of the paintings of Edward Hopper. Beatrice's world contrasts a tony architect's apartments with her own cramped flat and her mother's suburban house. Gene's world is neo-realist, all messy offices, busy diners and subways. Troy at first inhabits a world of clean offices, nice cars and expensive bars, but his slow fall robs him of his possessions and his sense of hope.

Beatrice's friend Dorrie is her Margaret equivalent, the rebel and nonconformist, yet even she withdraws from her best friend in the face of the injuries Beatrice endures. (Beatrice's case is a variation on an incident that Jill Sprecher herself endured: getting mugged in New York so severely that she had to undergo brain surgery.) When we first see this friend, who is also a co-worker, she is playing around in the apartment Beatrice is cleaning, at one point putting on a wig she finds. This foreshadows the wig that Beatrice's mother gives her after brain surgery. The linking of visual imagery makes solid and interconnected a world that seems to be coming apart for the characters themselves.

Perhaps the most poignant moment in the film occurs when Walker, the physics professor who is even more rigid than the managers of Global Credit, unhappily married and cheating on his wife, learns that one of his students has committed suicide. Walker realises that he is partially to blame: he's been difficult about the results of a test and unloaded on the boy after a particularly bad moment with his mistress, also a colleague in the university. Walker is passing out the results of a test, only to learn that the student is dead. Another student, off screen, reminds him that he had just been teaching the class about falling objects and their trajectories. For one fleeting second, the viewer can see that a small bit of humanity has redefined Walker's otherwise soulless physics.

The central question at the end of *Thirteen Conversations About One Thing* is, what is that 'thing' they are talking about? Possible answers, different for each viewer, could be 'life', 'happiness', or even 'suicide'. The film posits the question, 'How can we possibly be happy in a world in which life seems pointless and suicide the only answer?' That Jill and Karen Sprecher keep the actual 'conversation' vague gives them the latitude to explore myriad layers of contemporary human beings with roving curiosity. That their answer or answers to the questions are tentative, quiet and provisional, only contributes further to the solemn majesty of this modern master-piece.

## Interview with... Jill Sprecher

**What is your definition of independent cinema, if any?**
Good question. There was a time when 'independent' meant that a film's financing came from sources outside the established studio system. Then the studios opened specialty divisions to make riskier movies at lower budgets. Some of those 'smaller' movies seem to resemble less expensive versions of studio films. For me, the distinction is not simply financial; it's more about form and content. If a movie breaks some rules, or focuses on subject matter that might not seem obvious, or features characters that have been marginalised – anything that runs counter to what's considered mainstream – that is the hallmark of independence. Chances are, fewer hands have touched it, too. The development process, which can stretch out forever and has to accommodate numerous opinions, might tend to water things down.

**As a viewer do you distinguish between independent and commercial cinema?**
As a viewer, I want to see an interesting story that's well told. And ideally something I haven't seen too many times

before. I don't really care about the behind the scenes drama regarding how it got financed or how many times it was rejected; it's really what's on the screen that's important to me. Some of my favourite movies happen to be blockbusters and others remain way off the radar.

**Do you think of yourself as an independent filmmaker?**

It's pretty presumptuous of me to refer to myself as a filmmaker at all, having only made two films in the last ten years. I think of myself more as a writer; that is mainly how my sister and I earn a living. The filmmaking has really been an extension of the writing process. I ended up directing *Clockwatchers* by default, since we didn't have the connections to get our script to a real director. I'll admit it was nice to have some say over the material beyond the actual writing. Then I got spoiled, so directing *Thirteen Conversations* was something I hoped to do from the beginning of the script.

I identify more with the independent world than with mainstream Hollywood, for obvious reasons. We haven't really worked in the studio system at all. And not for lack of trying. We'd be happy to sell out, if we could find any takers.

**You and your sister co-produce your films. How much do you find you have to involve yourself with the money side of filmmaking?**

We were very involved in it, for both films. If you want to make something happen, you have to be involved, especially if it costs money. No one is going to fork it over. And it's a lot of money, even on low-budget movies. Getting the financing was definitely the hardest part of the filmmaking process, and the most time-consuming. We'd get someone to commit to financing, then approach actors, then the money would fall away, or an actor would become unavailable, and everything would start all over. But that's pretty much the norm on independent films. It's a juggling act. In the end, though, everything lined up the way it should have; we got the perfect cast for both movies and made the films we wanted to make.

**Do you think that you would ever be a filmmaker if the nature of the business had not changed significantly since the 1970s?**
The 1970s really represents my favourite period in American cinema. So many interesting stories came out of that era, and even the blockbusters had a very personal feel to them. Maybe it was due to the Vietnam War and the Watergate scandal; there was a real mistrust of government, and by extension big business. Some great paranoid thrillers were made, which I particularly love. Then things seemed to change in the 80s. Isn't that period referred to as the 'Me Decade'? That's when a lot of conspicuous wealth began to be rubbed in people's faces. Show business subsequently became more about the business than about the show. Weekend box office reports appeared in regular newspapers, not just the trades. Suddenly a movie's profits were newsworthy. I remember seeing Jean-Luc Godard being interviewed in a documentary, and he said something to the effect of, 'In the future, Hollywood

will only make one movie a year, and it will cost a fortune.' He wasn't too far off. But things happen in cycles, and the monolithic power of the studios is probably responsible in part for the rebirth of independent films. If you can't force your way into the system, you figure out a way to play outside it. I was definitely encouraged by the fact that little movies were being made right in my neighbourhood in New York. My sister and I both worked in production on a number of them before trying to do our own.

**What is the state of the art now and where do you see cinema going, both technically and in terms of content?**
The new technologies have certainly put moviemaking into the hands of a lot more individuals, which is nice. Digital video has lowered the cost, and the Internet and number of cable channels have increased the volume for 'product'. At the same time, it seems that fewer people are actually going to theatres to watch films. That is a little disheartening to me. I think movie-watching should be a communal event.

**What do you think of DVD technology? Why have so many filmmakers embraced that medium with so much more alacrity than VHS tapes? Or are you a technophobe?**
I must confess, I don't own a DVD player. But now that they're getting into my price range (under $100), I hope to own one soon. I think the clarity of the image is much better than video, and usually the DVDs keep the original format. (The video transfer of *Clockwatchers* was not supervised by me or the cinematographer, and conse-

quently is much brighter than how it was filmed.) Fortunately, Dick Pope, who shot *Thirteen Conversations,* supervised the transfer, and the finished product resembles the print. I'm into the idea of added footage and explanations at the end; I wish that had been available when I was studying film. I've got a lot of catching up to do.

**What is your participation in *Big Love*?**
My sister and I were producers and writers for the first season. We wanted to get our feet wet in the television world. The overall vision of the show really belonged to the creators. Naturally, we would love to have a show of our own. We've written a couple of pilots and we're waiting to see what happens. The great thing about television is that it's almost immediate. You can write something and have it in front of an audience in no time. None of this waiting around for years, trying to dig up financing.

**Are you finding television a congenial medium?**
It's been fun. And I'm glad that a lot of television shows are breaking new ground, both in storytelling and in content. Like *24*. I've heard good things about *Dexter*, a Showtime series. There are some really innovative shows hitting the airwaves. Very timely material, told in interesting ways.

**When you finally came to make a movie, did any aspect of the process take you by surprise?**
I'm struck by the fact that, no matter how carefully one

can plan, or how well one envisions the material, a movie ultimately takes on a life of its own. Fortunately for me, in both cases, the finished product turned out better than I could have imagined. I guess this is part of the alchemy of filmmaking: a ray of sunlight appears at an unexpected moment, an actor does something we could never have scripted. Of course, I've been lucky enough to work with great people, the best in the business. Dick Pope is an amazing cinematographer. And Stephen Mirrione, who I've worked with twice, has taught me so much about filmmaking. He's got a great sense of storytelling and performance; he always manages to find that small gesture or silent moment that speaks volumes. Which brings me to another thing that took me by surprise – how little of the dialogue that my sister and I so laboriously wrote was actually needed in both films. A testament to the actors. And to the fact that cinema is truly a visual medium.

Both *Clockwatchers* and *Thirteen Conversations* fall into a relatively recent genre I call, for want of a better phrase, 'heroic alienation'. After years of Hollywood more or less ignoring the 'working person', suddenly there have been numerous films about corporate life: *In the Company of Men*, *Office Space*, *Fight Club*, *American Beauty*, and among foreign films, *Time Out*. Most of these films aren't strictly 'Hollywood' product. What do you think is 'in the air' to cause these films to emerge?

It's interesting, now that you name the films, I do see a

kind of trend. I think traditionally, Hollywood movies tend to be 'bigger' in all respects. The kind of mundane, slice-of-life stories have been the domain of European and Japanese films. Two of my favourite films are *Il Posto* (not to be confused with *Il Postino*!) by Ermanno Olmi, and *Les bonnes femmes* by Claude Chabrol. I think they were in the back of my mind when we were writing *Clockwatchers,* although I haven't seen either in a very long time. I'm not sure why these kinds of stories are in vogue in the US now, though. Maybe it had something to do with the end of the millennium, people examining their daily existence. Or maybe there are just more working stiffs who have managed to sneak into the film business.

### Was the timeline of *Thirteen Conversations* easy to plot out?

The timeline of *Thirteen Conversations* was not difficult for us. We wrote the storylines separately, putting the major scenes on note cards. Then we looked for moments in each story that might be a good place to switch to another character, so that when the two stories abutted, they would make some kind of statement.

The finished film is quite a bit like the original script. We wanted to end where we began, in the bar, but we also wanted kind of a prologue and epilogue, which the Amy Irving story adds. During editing, many of the producers wanted to cut the opening scene between Amy and John Turturro; but we held on and fought for it, because it so perfectly sets the tone for the movie. I think they thought the movie had two opening scenes. My response was, 'So what?' Who said there has to be just one?!

Gene (Alan Arkin) changes subtly through the course of *Thirteen Conversations*; he becomes a kind of silent guardian angel to the optimistic guy, Smiley Bowman, whom he originally didn't like, in an unlikely and no doubt unintended allusion to *Magnificent Obsession*. Then he smiles at a stranger (Amy Irving) on the subway with no way of knowing how significantly he is contributing to her life and mood. Is the film ending on a note of optimism?

We intended for *Thirteen Conversations* to end on an optimistic note. A friend of mine who read the original script way back when thought the ending was practically Disney (for us), it was so upbeat! Of course, some people think the film is melancholy, but that wasn't the intention. Alan Arkin's character makes amends to Smiley Bowman, primarily out of guilt. We took that a step further with the ending, to have him do something selfless, with no baggage or strings attached or hidden agenda, which would signal a positive change for him. And, of course, to hint at how the small gesture might really make a difference to the recipient, especially because she is not expecting it.

I love the way that in *Clockwatchers* Iris (Toni Collette) is slowly stripped of all her friends and surroundings. The movement of the movie really does capture that life experience when everything begins rosy before slowly turning

**to crap. Of course we wouldn't have 'stories' if life weren't this way.**

I guess *Clockwatchers* is kind of the anti-female-bonding movie; instead of grouping together and empowering each other they feed on each other's neuroses. Karen and I wanted to do some things backwards. Like the usual 'whodunnit' starts with many 'suspects' and whittles them down to one; we sort of moved in the opposite direction.

We also wanted to move from a kind of talky beginning, to less and less dialogue as the story progressed and the communication broke down among the individuals. In the script, almost the entire third act is silent. Of course, when we went to edit the film, many of the silent sequences were cut. The first assembly of the film was nearly three hours. We finally decided that 96 minutes of nothing happening was probably the limit, in terms of what an audience would tolerate.

**There are some beautiful, sometimes surreal shots in *Clockwatchers,* of odd office moments that are actually perfectly realistic. When you write a screenplay are the two of you thinking 'visually' or do you come up with such images collaboratively on the set?**

Most of the 'odd office moments', as you put it, were indeed in the script, like Jamie Kennedy sniffing a magic marker (something I still do), Lisa Kudrow painting her nails with Liquid Paper and the like. Of course, the actors embellished what was on the page. Lisa decided that while she was doing her nails, her character would also be 'working on her accents'. I think in the script we wrote that Stanley

DeSantis, who plays the supply guardian, was linking paper clips together into a long chain; but Stanley felt it was 'wasteful' and outside his character, so he came up with the idea of linking marker tops together.

There was a moment after Parker gets a memo that makes her angry, we wrote something like, 'She tears it up with a flourish'. When we went to shoot, Parker rolled out of her cubicle on a chair, tore up the paper, and tossed it into the air like confetti. Perfect.

**Isn't a lot of the excitement of making a movie in thinking up the little details? Such as in *Clockwatchers*: the oppressive ironic counterpoint of the Muzak; the different watches the temps wear that help define these clock watchers; the way Iris and Cleo (Helen FitzGerald) are sort of rendered mirror images of each other?**

The fun is definitely in the details. We had a great time choosing the Muzak when we were editing *Clockwatchers*. Stephen Mirrione, our editor, and Karen and I spent so much time picking out the most obscure and perfect song for each cue, really great Muzak of all different styles. Then we went to license it, and it added up to something like a million dollars, which was most of our budget! So we found a composer, Joey Altruda, who wrote his own songs, inspired by what we had picked out.

We really depend on everyone working on the movie to add to the details. Our costume designer on *Clockwatchers*, Edi Giguere, really put a lot of time into choosing each character's watch. And the actors themselves went out and bought a lot of the items for their desks, so we can't claim credit for any of that.

In both *Clockwatchers* and *Thirteen Conversations* a woman has a hopeless crush on a boss figure, and innocent people are suspected of thievery. I'm sure these similarities are unconscious. As a writer, what preoccupies you the most? That certain key ideas and observations are rendered accurately? That everything makes sense? That the actors have good lines? That there aren't so many settings that you will go over budget? All of the above? Or none?

For us, the most important thing is that the audience care about the characters, that they understand them, and perhaps see a bit of themselves in them, even when they do negative things. The least important thing, for us, is dialogue. Of course, we spend hours labouring over the right words, but we're also looking for ways to get rid of it on the set.

I once saw Clea DuVall in person and she looked very different (small, slight) than she does on screen (big-boned and tall). How does a filmmaker accommodate such differences while planning and making a film?

Clea *is* very petite, indeed. She's had some butt-kicking roles on film [*Ghost Planet*], though, carrying machine guns and the like, which may be why seeing her in person was a bit of a shock. She's also very soft-spoken. My first meeting with her was over the phone, and I fell in love with her voice. I didn't actually meet her in person until she showed up for the filming. She is a real sweetheart, and a wonderful actress.

So far I haven't been too surprised by meeting the actors we've worked with in person; but I must say I was pleased to find that there were no 'star egos' with any of them. In terms of the difference between the screen and reality, as [cinematographer] Dick Pope says, 'Film is the great equalizer.' It can make a large room look small, or a small one large. That's a trick we made use of in *Clockwatchers*, for example. In the script, the setting was supposed to be a massive, Kafka-style office, with hundreds of anonymous desks. On our budget, we could afford six desks. We had to constantly move them around and shoot the small space from odd angles to fool people into thinking it was much bigger.

**Was there anything about the movie business itself that really took you by surprise once you got involved in it?**
I guess the most surprising thing about the movie business is how slowly it moves. Everything. It's strange. People have cell phones, they take meetings, they look really busy, but nothing gets done. Sort of like *Clockwatchers*. When we were trying to raise money for both movies, we would hear things like, 'It's January, everyone is at Sundance'. Then it was, 'It's April, everyone is getting ready for Cannes'. Or, 'August is a bad month. Nobody reads.' Nobody reads, period. You can't even hand someone a one-page written synopsis, you have to do a 'pitch' and try to act everything out. Which is difficult, if you're not an actor. My sister and I happen to be two of the laziest people we know. I guess we finally found an industry that moves slower than us.

Movies are so hard to make at every stage of the process, why would anyone want to make one? What is it that drives someone, in the face of monumental resistance, to assert that they have something to say and that the audience needs to listen?

A giant ego, of course. Actually, come to think of it, I don't really have that kind of urgency or drive. As I say, I'm pretty lazy. With both movies, my sister and I never really expected them to happen. They just kind of kept moving along. We were waiting both times for someone to stop us. (Not that people didn't try...) But once they started to snowball and others got involved, we felt a responsibility to keep everything going. It's only when we look back in retrospect that we can't believe we finished them.

So I guess I should change my answer, then, to pride. We were too stubborn, and embarrassed, to allow them to fall apart.

**There seems to be a vast gulf between successful and unsuccessful moviemakers. Yet once a filmmaker 'makes it' they seem to join a club where they all know each other and drop each other's names on DVD audio tracks. Do you feel as if you have entered a private club?**

I know the gulf you're talking about between 'successful' and 'unsuccessful'. We happen to be on the unsuccessful side of that chasm. I'm $150,000 in debt, which I won't be able to get rid of any time soon. When I started working in the film business, I was a gopher running errands for free. Many years later, I'm still working for free. I did not get paid to direct *Thirteen Conversations,* and my sister and I used our credit cards constantly. In a way, I don't really consider myself in the same business as the successful filmmakers. They exist in a different world, with assistants and paychecks and job offers. This does not mean, however, that I can't drop a few names, but that is mainly because, if you've been out there for a while, you run into the successful people at festivals, or work for them or something. So I'm sort of in the private club, just not as a full member.

**Given how much trouble they are to make, why make films, as opposed to writing novels or philosophical papers, or political pamphlets or poems?**
When I was younger I liked to write prose and poetry. Then in college and grad school I mostly wrote papers and essays. I always wanted to write a novel someday, but I don't have enough discipline. Writing is very solitary. It's a good thing I've got my sister as a scriptwriting partner. But even with the two of us, it still gets lonely. There are days when we never leave the house. At least when we're writing a script, we have the hope that it might get made into a movie and therefore give us a reason to leave the house. I like the collaborative aspect of moviemaking. That's really the fun part. It makes the labour of writing worth it. Because, for me at least, writing is indeed laborious. My brain actually hurts after a while when I'm really trying to use it.

**You might have had a career in academia rather than in cinema. In your experience, what are some similarities**

**and differences between those two worlds?**

I think if I had an academic job, I would be struggling in that arena too. It's just as competitive as the film business. And there is the same pressure to 'produce'. (What's the saying? Publish or perish?) The main difference would probably be that I wouldn't have to read criticism of my work. Although, maybe I'm wrong. Maybe there's some equally embarrassing form of evaluation.

**If you *had* become an academic, you would have been one of those people writing about and teaching books and/or films. Do you have any thoughts on the continuity between the creative and the critical act, if such there be?**

I think sometimes the critical act gets in the way of creativity. For me, anyway. When I first moved to New York, before I studied film, I loved movies. Then I started taking classes and began analysing why I loved them. Pretty soon I was picking everything apart. It kind of ruins the experience. I guess I'm like the John Turturro character, I have a tendency to overanalyse. I know this will sound like heresy, but I find that I don't enjoy movies as much as I used to. I've gone back to reading for enjoyment.

**Who is your favourite philosopher?**

In college I used to read a lot of the French existentialists. You could say that *Clockwatchers* was probably inspired by *Being and Nothingness.* I also like Bertrand Russell; one of his books [*The Conquest of Happiness*] was very helpful when we were writing *Thirteen Conversations.* My favourite contemporary philosopher would have to be Noam Chomsky. I've been reading a lot of his books lately. When I'm really depressed, though, I read Viktor Frankl. Technically, he's not a philosopher, but *Man's Search For Meaning* is one of the best books ever written about what's truly important.

**What would you do if you received a MacArthur 'genius' grant, as John Sayles did?**

I'm not in danger of winning a MacArthur grant. Which is probably a good thing. It's supposed to be 'free money', but I wouldn't think of it that way. Can you imagine the pressure of trying to create something of 'genius' calibre? Even though I'm broke, I don't like the idea of being paid in advance for something. That happened to me once. It created it's own special hell. I couldn't even think, it was like my brain purposely shut down.

**Why don't you and Karen cast yourselves in little bit parts in your own movies the way other directors do?**

Karen and I are two of the most self-conscious people we know. We have no business being in front of a camera. And I'd like to extend that to having my voice recorded, which, if you get the DVD, you'll understand why. I'm still astounded every time I hear my nasal Midwestern twang played back and can't believe that's what I sound like. It's very offensive. I did manage to rope Karen into filling an empty chair in John Turturro's classroom since we were short on extras that day. She was terrified. John kept threatening to call on her. Later she told me she felt she 'overacted', which seems impossible, given that she was just sitting in a chair. So she's not comfortable being in the spotlight at all.

## Are your screenplays ever going to be published?

As far as I know, the screenplays are not going to be published. Which is probably a good thing, since Karen and I don't own them anymore, and it would just piss us off.

# INDEPENDENT CINEMA AS STEPPING STONE: JAMES MANGOLD

In the 1970s, it was a joke, a teen's common response when questioned on their choice of career: 'What I really want to do is direct'. It even showed up as a catch phrase on a t-shirt in Alan Arkin's hilarious adaptation of the Jules Feiffer play, *Little Murders* (1971).

Back in those days, entry into the movie business, though always difficult, was sometimes helped by making an attention-grabbing short film; with luck a new director could win an award at a film festival or have his/her film picked up for circulation by one of the short film distributors. Steven Spielberg and John Carpenter, for example, both took this route. Working in a Roger Corman company was another good option. Later, in the 1980s, it was fashionable to craft a horror film. They tended to be relatively easy to finance because they usually make back their investment. Despite the subject-matter, struggling actors were also happy to appear and thus get paid for their work. Crucially, the genre encourages a dynamic visual style, perfect for a budding director who wants to show off his imagination.

In the 1990s, however, another possibility opened up. This option consisted of making a so-called 'independent film', shepherding it through the festivals, and with luck selling it to a studio. With this 'track record', it was then possible for a director to swing a deal for future work with a studio. The overriding impulse of such filmmakers is to enter the studio system, not maintain their 'independence', perhaps under the belief that they could bend the studios to their will, which one or two directors a generation in fact do manage to do, such as David O Russell, who went from *Spanking the Monkey* (1994) to *Three Kings* (1999), Christopher Nolan, who went from *Following* (1996) to *Memento* (2000) to *Batman Begins* (2003), and Doug Liman, who went from making indie-style features such as *Swingers* (1996) and *Go* (1999) to helming big-budget action pics *The Bourne Identity* (2002) and *Mr and Mrs Smith* (2005). Meanwhile, the majority of filmmakers tagged with the indie label, such as Gregg Araki and Guy Maddin, prefer to remain miniaturists.

Many books and articles have already been written about the rise of the film festival circuit and the increasing importance of the Telluride festival, held in a skiing community in Colorado, and then the Sundance festival, in Utah, in encouraging alternatives to mainstream Hollywood moviemaking. Briefly, the Telluride Film Festival held its inaugural event in 1974. Then, as now, it simply shows movies, usually around 30, to paying attendees, generally industry insiders. Among the many films that made their debut at Telluride are *Sling Blade* (1996) and *Lost in Translation* (2003). The festival specialises in independent films. As at Sundance, however, bidding wars can erupt between small distributors over unattached films.

Sundance began life as the USA Film Festival in 1978, with the purpose of encouraging film production in Utah. Its guardian angel is the actor Robert Redford, who renamed the festival after the real-life character he once played. Like the Telluride festival, Sundance is famous for promoting independent films but is a bigger, more sprawling festival that gives a cavalcade of prizes, and also holds workshops in which aspiring filmmakers can toil on their scripts in collaboration with the Hollywood elite. Quentin Tarantino, for example, 'workshopped' *Reservoir Dogs* at Sundance, and the finished film played in the festival a year later. And like Telluride, it is an unofficial film market, where studios compete with each other for distribution rights, sometimes as a movie is still screening.

Telluride and especially Sundance became an important component in the rise of the independent film, and in the 1990s was an essential launching pad for filmmakers such as Tarantino and David O Russell, to the 'major motion picture' world. Others include Alexander Rockwell, Gregg Araki, Allison Anders, Larry Clark, Terry Zwigoff and Todd Haynes.

One such filmmaker is James Mangold. But Mangold had an interesting career even before he entered the world of indie film production. Born in New York City in 1963, he was raised in upstate New York by his artist parents. He attended the California Institute for the Arts, the Disney studio-sponsored college in Southern California, where he studied under the film director-turned-teacher Alexander MacKendrick, best known for the noir classic *Sweet Smell of Success* (1957), the quintessential Ealing comedies *The Ladykillers* (1955) and *The Man in the White Suit* (1951), and the kid's film *A High Wind in Jamaica* (1965).

Mangold attracted attention at CalArts and ended up working at Disney at the age of 21, in large part thanks to a short film he made, called *Barn*. Like the short films made by other directors, it was cynically designed to show off his directing skills. In fact, Mangold told *Creative Screenwriting* magazine in a 2006 podcast that he designed *Barn* with the idea of accomplishing six goals in mind, among them achieving high production values from limited resources, and creating a sequence showing parallel action, reasoning that, 'If I did these six things I'd get hired by everybody. And I did'.

At Disney, Mangold went on to write the animated film *Oliver and Company* (1988). But, as he has frankly discussed in interviews, Mangold was not happy in the corporate climate of the Disney studio, and in a bold move, returned to college, entering the film school at Columbia. There he wrote the screenplay to his directorial debut, *Heavy* (1995), which won the best directing prize at Sundance. This film led to a deal with Miramax to make a long-cherished project, *Cop Land* (1997). With his next film, *Girl, Interrupted* (1999), Mangold entered the realm of elite Hollywood directors who could lead performers to Oscar awards, with Angelina Jolie winning a Best Supporting Actress Award. Reese Witherspoon later won a Best Actress Oscar as June Carter Cash in *Walk the Line* (2003); indeed almost all of Mangold's films have won or been nominated for awards.

Mangold has used his increasing prestige in Hollywood to do something unusual, mounting versions of almost every standard film genre. Thus far he has made a drama, a crime film, a romantic comedy, a coming-of-age tale, a thriller, a musical and/or biopic, and a western. With this penchant for, and sweeping ability to make, numerous genres, he most resembles Howard Hawks (1896–1977). Hawks was so versatile he could conceive everything from shark attack movies to road race movies, in addition to the more commonplace westerns and comedies. It is arguable that Hawks, as Robin Wood has pointed out, made the best screwball comedy (*Twentieth Century* [1934]), the best gangster film (*Scarface* [1932]), the best western (*Rio Bravo* [1959]), and the best science-fiction film (*The Thing From Another World* [1951], on which he's credited as producer) from Hollywood's so-called classical period. Yet there is thematic and stylistic consistency throughout all these diverse films. In modern filmmaking it is more difficult to maintain a consistent visual style across diverse films, but Mangold has certain settings and camera uses that he favours, and his films contain thematic concerns which link them all.

While approaching Hollywood and making movies on his own terms in genres reminiscent of Hollywood's heyday, Mangold has also managed to introduce facets of the indie world into his films. He has drawn on unusual actors such as Pruitt Taylor Vince and elicited remarkable performances. He has taken the 'novelty casting' of independent features to an extreme, compiling interesting collections of actors that appear at odds with each other (Sylvester Stallone and

Harvey Keitel), and emphasised indie film's strong suit, character and dialogue, over action and special effects.

What Mangold has lacked over the course of his career, however, is a consistent confederacy of collaborators. Except for Vince, Ray Liotta and Robert Patrick, Mangold has rarely worked with the same people through several films. One lesson that the careers of directors such as John Ford and Martin Scorsese has taught is that consistent collaborators are a plus when it comes to inscribing your vision on film. Mangold's choice of behind-the-scenes crew would suggest that he has finally found his career collaborators: he has now made two movies with cinematographer Phedon Papamichael, and four with editor Michael McCusker.

## *Heavy* (1995)

**Directed by:** James Mangold
**Written by:** James Mangold
**Produced by:** Richard Miller
**Edited by:** Meg Reticker
**Cinematography:** Michael Barrow
**Cast:** Pruitt Taylor Vince (Victor Modino), Shelley Winters (Dolly Modino), Liv Tyler (Callie), Deborah Harry (Delores), Leo (Joe Grifasi)

Victor Modino is an older overweight man still living with his widowed mother and cooking at *Pete and Dolly's*, the diner in the Hudson Valley that his mother owns. The only other employee is Delores, a waitress. While Dolly sits in the kitchen in a huge, worn easy chair, Delores (who once had an affair with Pete) desultorily flirts with wizened regular Leo, and the near-silent Victor makes the pizzas. When Dolly hires the college dropout Callie to fill in, she unintentionally creates an atmosphere of frustration and desire, as Delores feels threatened, and Victor feels long-suppressed yearnings. When Dolly dies, Victor keeps it a secret, stuck in the routine of making her breakfast every morning, while having dreams of 'rescuing' Callie. Eventually, Victor's passion compels him to speak, if not to Callie, then to someone.

*Heavy* betrays its indie roots in its unusual casting and the cost-saving strategy of setting its events primarily in one robust location. A quiet, almost contemplative look at ordinary people, it also emphasises character over action.

The central characters of *Heavy* are based on real people whom Mangold observed in his hometown in upstate New York. Yet at the same time, Victor Modino reflects something of Mangold himself, who, as he has admitted in interviews, was at a low point in his career and self-esteem when the concept of *Heavy* came to him. Mangold not only uses the characters in the film to reflect on his reality, he also uses them to reflect on each other's reality. For example, Victor is contrasted with barfly Leo. Both pine after a woman. Both spend untold hours in the same place. Yet the subtle differences between them (one is noisy, the other silent; one is at the threshold of his life, the other at the twilight) help give a character-driven film a narrative momentum.

Billy Wilder once advised, 'Let your objects tell the story'. Few films follow that precept, however. One exception is Terrence Malick's *Days of Heaven* (1978), a mostly visual film. Another is *Heavy*; reviewers noted that Mangold's film is nearly silent. The objects in Victor's world tell us all we need to know about his opinions, fears, hopes: the worn chair his mother is planted in, the delicacy with which he prepares her breakfast plate; and then the chaos that ensues in his home kitchen after her death. Taught to observe by the film's own strategies, the viewer comes away with a ray of hope for Victor when he appears to make human contact with a convenience store employee.

A one-time student of MacKendrick, Mangold may himself end up a great teacher. The introductions to his published screenplays, usually in interview form, are masterclasses in film practice and theory. But though Mangold is hyperaware of how films work and can articulate his insights, his films do not have the rigid formalism of other filmmaking intellectuals. They move, they breathe, they interact with the viewer.

Words like 'small', 'quiet' and 'intimate' are used to describe *Heavy*. Like *Barn*, the film accomplished its mission, launching Mangold into a legitimate commercial filmmaking career. But *Heavy* is not a heartless exercise in plot points and virtuosity. It's a heartfelt examination of ordinary people that takes what indie films do best and excels at it.

## *Cop Land* (1997)

**Directed by:** James Mangold
**Written by:** James Mangold
**Produced by:** Cathy Konrad, Ezra Swerdlow, Cary Woods
**Edited by:** Craig McKay
**Cinematography:** Eric Edwards
**Cast:** Sylvester Stallone (Sheriff Freddy Heflin), Harvey Keitel (Ray Donlan), Ray Liotta (Gary 'Figgsy' Figgis), Robert De Niro (Lt Moe Tilden), Peter Berg (Joey Randone), Janeane Garofalo (Deputy Cindy Betts), Robert Patrick (Jack Rucker), Michael Rapaport (Murray 'Superboy' Babitch), Annabella Sciorra (Liz Randone), Noah Emmerich (Deputy Bill Geisler), Cathy Moriarty (Rose Donlan), John Spencer (Leo Crasky), Edie Falco (Berta)

Freddy Heflin is the sheriff of Garrison, a New Jersey town just on the other side of Manhattan, off the George Washington Bridge. Ray Donlan, a NYC cop with links to mobsters, and the town's unofficial leader, installed Freddy in the job. Freddy has always wanted to be a 'real' cop, but a youthful injury to his ear while rescuing the town beauty, Liz, has left him partially deaf and unfit for police work. When Ray's nephew, Murray, another officer, is involved in a shooting, his apparent suicide seems to close the matter. But Freddy knows that Murray is still alive, and in hiding in Garrison. In order to maintain a fiction, Ray needs to kill Murray, while Freddy, tired of being caretaker of the increasingly volatile town, wants to deliver Murray to the internal investigation unit of the New York Police, led by Ray's old nemesis Moe.

A measure of a strong script is that everyone wants to do it, and there are so many roles in *Cop Land* that Mangold was able to raid the top actors of the period, along with future standouts, such as Edie Falco in a minor part.

*Cop Land* is almost a life's work. Its roots stretch back to childhood, when Mangold was raised in a 'white flight' city in upstate New York and pondered the lives of people who work for and defend one city but live in another. Almost novelistic in its complexity and multi-layering, *Cop Land* is a condensed, compact tale that follows an ordinary person to an emotional breakthrough. Freddy is this film's Victor, an overweight, disregarded, underestimated person who reaches a crisis point and resolves to resist his fate. He is another one of Mangold's dense, isolated characters coming to an understanding about himself and his society. Unlike *Heavy*, however, *Cop Land* has villains. Keitel's hard cop who has forged a haven for his colleagues is a precursor to Vic Mackey on the FX television series *The Shield*, a man who will do anything to defend his turf, even if it means killing some of those same colleagues.

But as much as *Cop Land* is Freddy's story it is also Figgis's tale. A parallel creation, an undercover cop disparaged by his fellow officers due to complex incidents in the film's backstory, Figgis too must make a decision that will change his life: stay and help Freddy and betray his friends, or flee with the insurance money he has defrauded? *Cop Land* opens with Figgis helping an intoxicated, off-duty

Freddy walk to his car; the film ends with Figgis helping him walk the distance to the NYPD headquarters.

Ray Liotta's Figgis is just one of a wealth of great performances in *Cop Land*, from Stallone down (cult lovers of the film relish Liotta's 'cleansing' speech to Stallone). Particularly effective is Keitel's Ray Donlan. The look of contempt he gives his rival Moe, played by Robert De Niro, is priceless.

*Cop Land* is famously but unofficially based on the Delmer Daves western *3:10 to Yuma*, released in 1957, and itself based on an Elmore Leonard novel. Freddy's last name is a homage to the lead actor in the film, Van Heflin. 2007 saw the release of Mangold's *official* remake of *Yuma*, starring Russell Crowe and Christian Bale. As in *Cop Land*, the Daves-Leonard *Yuma* concerns an ordinary man called upon to perform extraordinary tasks, with a small measure of the kind of internal family tension found in George Stevens's *Shane* (1953), in which Van Heflin's Joe Starrett feels compelled to prove himself to his son. *Cop Land* is a better movie than Daves's *Yuma*; more expansive and more poignant in its portrait of a truly isolated person.

### *Walk the Line* (2005)

**Directed by:** James Mangold
**Written by:** Gill Dennis, James Mangold
**Produced by:** Cathy Konrad, James Keach
**Edited by:** Michael McCusker
**Cinematography:** Phedon Papamichael

**Cast:** Joaquin Phoenix (Johnny Cash), Reese Witherspoon (June Carter), Ginnifer Goodwin (Vivian Cash), Robert Patrick (Ray Cash), Dallas Roberts (Sam Phillips)

As country and western star Johnny Cash is about to return to the stage to finish his show in Folsom Prison, he lingers in the woodworking room, his eyes alighting on the blade of a table saw. This evokes for him memories of his childhood, in which his brother was always viewed as the 'good son' by his withdrawn, ungiving father. After a stint in the army, Cash marries and pursues a career as a singer while selling merchandise door to door. An audition with prominent record mogul Sam Phillips leads to a recording contract and a modest career. On the road in a revue with other rising stars Cash falls in love with June Carter. Although she reciprocates his feelings, she spurns him, and Cash, unable to handle fame, slips into drugs and drink, ruining potential future tours. Eventually, June Carter and her family help Cash overcome his addiction and, while on the road again, he proposes to her on stage and she finally accepts. Back in the present, Cash returns to the stage and rouses the audience of convicts with more songs, as June looks on admiringly.

On the American PBS chat show *Charlie Rose* (5 April 2007), director Quentin Tarantino made a confession: 'If there is one genre I think is the disreputable genre out there, that I never want to have anything to do with it, it's the biopic. I can't stand the biopics. They're all just showcases for actors who want awards, mostly because they want to do this story from beginning to end.' Having said that, Tarantino went on to admit that he might some day shoot the life story of John Brown. There is a whole array of quasi-secret dream projects that directors harbour; usually biopics of figures with whom they identify, such as Sylvester Stallone and Edgar Alan Poe. *Walk the Line* was a project that Mangold wanted to make as far back as *Cop Land*. It might have been his third film had not events, in the typical way they happen in Hollywood, intervened to delay its production.

So why Cash? At the time, when Cash was still alive, country and western music had become corporatised. Mangold, a music nut (as many good directors are or have to be), revered Cash as an American original. Making the movie would be an act of celebration, and a rebuke to fake contemporary country and western music. But did Mangold, on some level, identify with Cash? It's easy to contrive parallels. For example, both Cash, at least in the film, and Mangold, came from reasonably humble origins to break into a competitive business. Like Cash, Mangold also had a career crisis that compelled him to return to his roots.

Thus, in the best tradition of indie spirit, Mangold managed to take an established genre and turn it into a personal enterprise, making a quiet chamber piece that reflected his own life and crises while officially making a big-budget film with popular stars.

In his quest to conquer all of Hollywood's film genres, Mangold made one of the best examples of an otherwise degraded quasi-genre. While contemporary filmmakers may find themselves inhibited, striving for fidelity to the facts of their subjects' lives, in the so-called classical era of the Hollywood system, the studios would simply make things up to fill gaps. The film biography of Cole Porter, *Night and Day* (1946), starring Cary Grant, is almost wholly fiction; and Samuel Fuller admits to creating details for his western *I Shot Jesse James* (1949). Mangold, however, managed to make an exemplary biopic by ignoring the source autobiographies, which obfuscated the stars' lives, and drawing the real stories out of Johnny Cash and June Carter during conversations and interviews with them. In the transformation, Mangold managed to remain faithful to Cash's life while also highlighting aspects of the musician's life that reflect his own crises.

# INDEPENDENT CINEMA AS AUTOBIOGRAPHY: WHIT STILLMAN

'Quirkiness' is one of the key terms used to define independent cinema. For example, an independent film thinks nothing of pausing while its characters discuss a trivial facet of popular culture. A famous example would be Quentin Tarantino's *Reservoir Dogs*, in which gangsters driving to a briefing about a jewellry store heist lapse into a discussion of TV shows such as *Get Christie Love*. In *Pulp Fiction*, John Travolta's character delineates the subtle differences between MacDonalds' food in America and Europe. The purpose of such scenes, at least on the script level, is to make the villainous characters seem recognisably human; showing them debating the same trivial subjects in popular culture that the educated film fan watching the movie is likely to discuss. Since the appearance of those two movies, virtually every independent film with a crime-based story has utilised the trick of a long walk-and-talk conversation in which rogues portray their in-depth knowledge of TV shows, board games, movies and music.

There is a curious moment in Whit Stillman's *The Last Days of Disco* where Josh (Matt Keeslar) falls into a debate in the middle of a disco night on the relative merits of Tramp, the Disney animated-movie character, versus Scotty. What's unusual about this sequence is not that it takes place in an ostensibly independent film but that it occurs in a Whit Stillman movie. Not commonly associated with pop culture, his films are usually free of the taint of modernity. None of his movies take place in the 'present'. They are nearly always set in the recent past. The characters conduct themselves with a great deal of seriousness, and think hard about their lives. There is a certain level of good-natured, knowing character mockery, but not on the level of a Woody Allen film in which he examines the same social class – in *Interiors*, say, or *Hannah and Her Sisters*. Allen's social elites are desiccated, selfish people, hypocrites angling for self-preservation. For Stillman, his characters are the last vestiges of true civilisation. Stillman is one of the few sympathetic observers on screen of what can only be called 'nerd' traits, such as interpersonal awkwardness, while celebrating other aspects of that culture, in particular in-depth knowledge of obscure subjects. He is a proponent of happy endings, and an advocate of a true conservative philosophy of social hierarchies. When he cites a Disney film, you know that it is absolutely pertinent to his meaning and the film's milieu.

Whit Stillman was born in Washington, DC in 1952. His father was active in the Democratic Party, working for congressman FDR, Jr, while in his career Stillman has been associated with conservative publications. He graduated from Harvard in 1973, intending to become a novelist, but found the life isolating. He worked as an editorial assistant

Chloe Sevigny as Alice Kinnon & Chris Eigeman as Des McGrath in *The Last Days of Disco* (1998), Dir. Whit Stillman. Grammercy Pictures/Photofest

Deborah Harry in *Heavy* (1985), Dir. James Mangold. Columbia Tristar/Photofest

Sylvester Stallone (as Sheriff Freddy Heflin), Robert De Niro (as Lt. Moe Tilden) in *Cop Land* (1997), Dir. James Mangold. Miramax/Buena Vista Pictures/Photofest

David Fox (as Fyodor Kent, Mark McKinney (as Chester Kent), Ross McMillan (as Roderick Kent) in *The Saddest Music in the World* (2004), Dir. Guy Maddin. IFC Films/Photofest

Jamie Kennedy, Parker Posey, Toni Collette, Lisa Kudrow, Alanna Ubach, Debra Jo Rupp in *Clockwatchers* (1998), Dir. Jill Sprecher. Artistic Licence/Photofest

Taylor Nichols, Chris Eigeman in *Barcelona* (1994), Dir. Whit Stillman. Fine Line Features/Photofest

Maya Deren in *Meshes of the Afternoon* (1943), Dirs. Maya Deren, Alexander Hammid. Photofest

Matthew McConaughey as guilt-ridden prosecutor Troy in *Thirteen Conversations About One Thing* (2001), Dir. Jill Sprecher.

John Turturro as Professor Walker in a Hopperesque moment from *Thirteen Conversations About One Thing* (2001), Dir. Jill Sprecher.

New guy Gregg (Kelly Miller) in *New Guy*, Dir. Bilge Ebiri, 2003, Siete Machos Films.

Vince Mola as George Walker, Mary Monahan as Mary Sherman in *Head Trauma*. Copyright: Martin M. Pepe & Jack Bromiley/Head Trauma LLC, 2006.

Gary 'Figgsy' Figgis (Ray Liotta) and Sheriff Freddy Heflin (Sylvester Stallone) in *Cop Land* (1997), Dir. James Mangold.

Audrey Rouget (Carolyn Farina) and Jane Clark (Allison Parisi) explain the ways of the world to Tom Townsend (Edward Clements) in *Metropolitan* (1990), Dir. Whit Stillman.

Isabella Rossellini (as Lady Port-Huntly) in *The Saddest Music in the World* (2004 Canada), Dir. Guy Maddin. IFC Films/Photofest

at a publishing firm (an experience that must have contributed to his view of publishing in *The Last Days of Disco*), then became a Barcelona-based foreign sale agent for Spanish films, where he also acted in a couple of movies, before returning to New York to head a cartoonist agency. While running the agency, Stillman wrote *Metropolitan*, which was released in 1990. He has since made only two more films, *Barcelona* in 1994 and *The Last Days of Disco* in 1998. As of this writing, Stillman is directing an adaptation of Christopher Buckley's novel *Little Green Men*.

Throughout this career, Stillman has contributed to various publications, sometimes under a pseudonym, including *Harper's*, *The Village Voice*, the *Guardian*, the *American Spectator* and the *Wall Street Journal*. Stillman once told this author during a conventional interview during the promotion of *Barcelona* that his choice of publication was based almost solely on the level of interference from editors: he said he hated being edited. Stillman's ambition to become a novelist was partially realised with the 2000 publication of *The Last Days of Disco, With Cocktails at Petrossian Afterwards*, which is his personal contribution to the genre of movie novelisations.

Stillman's movies have been made outside the mainstream. While working in Spain's film industry, he picked up some hints and techniques about how to build financing and employed them to get *Metropolitan* off the ground. He incorporated the production company and sold shares to his friends and their families, raising $200,000. The film was shot in and around Manhattan in 1989, often without permits. For example, in some scenes characters are shown walking into or out of a hotel or bar but the subsequent interiors were photographed elsewhere. The script for *Metropolitan* took four years to write; Stillman conceived of *Barcelona* originally in 1983, and took a decade to finalise it. After the success of *Metropolitan*, he has (or had) a first-look arrangement with Castle Rock, which produced his next two films. A small UK-based production company called Golconda is producing *Little Green Men*.

Stillman insists that his characters be literate, articulate, concerned and caring, and slightly at odds with the world of wealth they inhabit. These qualities set him apart from the vast run of independent films, which tend to dwell more on working-class men and women, on criminals, college students, expatriates and immigrants, and 'ordinary' families. Whit Stillman is 'independent' in any business definition of the word, but not in content.

### *Metropolitan* (1990)

**Directed by:** Whit Stillman
**Written by:** Whit Stillman
**Produced by:** Whit Stillman, Peter Wentworth
**Edited by:** Christopher Tellefsen
**Cinematography:** John Thomas
**Cast:** Carolyn Farina (Audrey Rouget), Edward Clements (Tom Townsend), Christopher Eigeman (Nick Smith), Taylor Nichols (Charlie Black), Allison Parisi (Jane Clark), Dylan Hundley (Sally Fowler), Bryan Leder (Fred Neff), Will Kempe

(Rick Von Sloneker), Elizabeth Thompson (Serena Slocum), Roger W Kirby (Man at Bar, Dick Edwards)

During the debutante season in Manhattan high society in the holiday weeks between college semesters, Tom Townsend falls in with a group of girls and their public escorts. Among them is Audrey Rouget, who has had a crush on Tom since college, though all the uptight young man – who hides from the others his reduced circumstances and the divorce of his parents – can talk about is his relationship with his ex-girlfriend, Serena. Meanwhile, Charlie, who is in love with Audrey, views Tom as a threat, and Nick, the most vibrant raconteur of the lot, takes Tom under his wing. When it is almost too late, Tom realises that he does love Audrey, and he and Charlie go on a rescue mission to Long Island in order to save her from the clutches of a crass aristocrat.

Mose Harper, the aged hanger-on in John Ford's film *The Searchers*, is famous for being characterised by John Wayne's Ethan Edwards as someone who was 'born old'. Whit Stillman was born old. All three of his films highlight the values of an older society or civilisation, and *Metropolitan* risks dismissal from the same quarters that reject Woody Allen's films for their emphasis on social elites.

However, there's a practical reason for setting a story among aristocrats. Freed from the necessity of showing how people make a living, the filmmaker can concentrate on the tender lines of passion that arise among different people.

*Metropolitan* also captures the dissipation, the intellectual ambition, the detachment, the snobbism (unconscious or not), the secret lives, and the biting sarcasm among jobless college students between seasons as it tells an Austen-like tale of love and social climbing during the Christmas and debutant season in Manhattan sometime in the 1980s.

The central character is Tom Townsend (Edward Clements), an interloper who becomes a sort of debutante escort despite being an intellectual radical. He gives the viewer entry into the world of the film. The post-collegial set he gets involved with is the SFRP, or Sally Fowler Rat Pack, which includes Nick (Christopher Eigeman), his Charon into this group and its society.

Tom makes a telling admission to Jane Austen-obsessed Audrey. He doesn't really read novels; he reads the criticism of them, simultaneously benefitting from the summarised story and the views of the critic on the book. This is how Tom lives his life, two steps away from everything. He is barred somewhat from the SFRP by his reduced circumstances: his father is rich but his mother, with whom he lives, is on a fixed income. His political views clash with the goals of an aristocratic society yet he continues to be fascinated by the Rat Pack, whilst never fully admitting it to himself. And in his anthropological foray into the Rat Pack and the debutante season, he studies the girls as he studies novels, with Nick Smith as the 'critic' who guides him through the narrative with helpful commentary, asides and footnotes. Despite their differences, Nick gives Tom the gift of reintegration into the society he should, by rights, be banished from.

Stillman's nostalgia for the recent past is a conserver's wish to honour values he feels are evaporating in the modern world. Furthermore, the viewers can still remember them.

*Metropolitan* is wonderfully well written and acted (*really* acted, by the way: Stillman and some of the other film-makers are at pains to explain on the audio commentary track on the Criterion DVD that only a couple of the people in the film are associated with the upper-class society that Stillman portrays). *Metropolitan* was well received by critics but also disparaged as right-wing, post-Reagan nostalgia with no story to speak of. In fact the film does have a story, but it also enjoys lovingly (though not uncritically) examining its characters, who drive the plot in a way that brings reality to the settings and motivations. The story is Proust-lite, in that we meet the characters, grow to enjoy their social set, and then see it evaporate under the feet of Tom as the times change and people move on.

### *Barcelona* (1994)

**Directed by:** Whit Stillman
**Written by:** Whit Stillman
**Produced by:** Whit Stillman
**Edited by:** Christopher Tellefsen
**Cinematography:** John Thomas
**Cast:** Taylor Nichols (Ted Boynton), Chris Eigeman (Fred Boynton), Tushka Bergen (Montserrat Raventos), Mira

Sorvino (Marta Ferrer), Thomas Gibson (Dickie Taylor), Jack Gilpin (The Consul)

Ted, an American living and working for an American-based corporation in Barcelona, receives a visit from his rambunctious cousin Fred, a naval officer on a mission as an advance man for a forthcoming visit by the US Sixth Fleet. Fred rouses Ted out of a certain lethargy and they begin to date various women, one of whom, Marta, steals money from him. Ted is also worried that the arrival of another executive from the Chicago office means that his job is doomed. While taking a cab to the airport, Fred is shot by anti-American activists and Ted nurses him back to health with the help of a trade-show girl he then falls in love with and marries.

There are two kinds of dictionaries in the world, the descriptive and the prescriptive. Descriptive dictionaries, like the current Webster's 3rd, merely state what words are currently in use, and make no pretence to guide the user to proper usage. The prescriptive dictionary is there to tell what is right and wrong. It will include a word that is deemed improper English, but label it nonstandard, vulgar, dialect or illiterate.

Whit Stillman's films are prescriptive. At root, they are lessons in how life should be lived, case studies in appropriate conduct, anthologies of proper values. In *Barcelona*, the Bible, Benjamin Franklin and Dale Carnegie are the touchstones of correct behaviour. Ted's behaviour is impeccable, and he constantly monitors himself and seeks self-improvement.

Ted is contrasted with his cousin Fred, a naval officer. Fred is reckless, a leach, opportunistic and blessed with a con man's gift of the gab, especially when he is defending himself against yet another one of Ted's complaints. He is fiercely patriotic, and resents the charge of fascism hurled at him by passers-by, and even attempts to rewrite an anti-American graffito.

The apotheosis of Fred's blithe unwillingness to fit in comes when he circumvents a debate Ted is having at a picnic with a friend of Montserrat. Fred smashes the anthill that Ted is trying to use as an example. Later Ted complains that, 'In one stupid move you confirm their worst assumptions'. Ted replies, 'I did not confirm their worst assumptions. I *am* their worst assumption'.

Ted tries to fit in agreeably, although he really can't. Ted is a Christian at odds with a godless society, one where Montserrat can say, 'All the old gods are dead. There is no god. That we know'. If Fred is a slight parody of the ugly American, brashly knocking down a civilisation he doesn't understand, then the godless Europe is a parody of the Jamesian 'old world' that mocks those *nouveau riche* Americans with shabby clothes and outmoded beliefs who are unable to keep up with the sophisticated society they bumble into.

Having lived in Spain for many years in the 1980s, and now living in France, Stillman knows European culture well, and also that parody doesn't stand up to reality. But here it suits his purpose, which is to contrast Ted and Fred's different attitudes to 'fitting in'.

The promise of *Metropolitan* was thoroughly fulfilled in

*Barcelona.* Though Stillman had aligned himself with a Hollywood production company, he managed to bring his vision to the screen, with all of its quirkiness, its violations of the rules of screenplay writing, as enunciated by screenwriting gurus such as Syd Field, and with character types who hitherto had not found their way to the screen. It's a slender tale with slight, if lovable, characters; far from the dynamic sort of film that even so-called independent film producers of the 21st century favour. But Stillman manages to pull it off, essentially through the strength of his vision, something very hard to hold on to amid the vagaries of movie production.

### *The Last Days of Disco* (1998)

**Directed by:** Whit Stillman
**Written by:** Whit Stillman
**Produced by:** Anthony Anderson, Jan Chapman
**Edited by:** Andrew Hafitz, Jay Pires
**Cinematography:** John Thomas
**Cast:** Chloë Sevigny (Alice Kinnon), Kate Beckinsale (Charlotte Pingress), Chris Eigeman (Des McGrath), Mackenzie Astin (Jimmy Steinway), Matt Keeslar (Josh Neff), Robert Sean Leonard (Tom Platt), Jennifer Beals (Nina Moritz), Burr Steers (Van)

The lives of various young socialites and yuppies intersect in a popular disco modeled on Studio 54. Among them are Alice, a shy woman who has trouble with men, her college and work friend Charlotte, essentially a conniving drama queen, and various men Des, who works at the disco, Jimmy Steinway, who dates Charlotte for a time, and Josh, a lawyer with the Department of Justice, which has been clandestinely investigating the disco via the entry given him by Jimmy and his ad agency. Josh helps shut down the disco and the group splits up to follow different paths.

Stillman did something unusual with the book version of his third film, *The Last Days of Disco*: two years after the film's release, he published a 'novelisation' bearing the elongated title *The Last Days of Disco, With Cocktails at Petrossian Afterwards*. Novelisations are a bastard industry in publishing, a strange marriage of moviemaking and book publishing. Generally, writers-for-hire are engaged to convert the script into a readable narrative, and are given some latitude to delve into the characters' minds in the manner of paperback original pulp fiction. Novelisations have some value for film criticism, however, because they can offer versions of the movie that have been discarded in the making but explain certain cruxes: plot points or character detail. A good example is the novelisation of Brian DePalma's *Snake Eyes*, which suffered an ending change during production that is still found in the novelisation, based on an early draft of the script. Some novelisations are even collectable, such as the book based on the script to John Carpenter's *Halloween*. Writers can take novelisations very seriously. The adaptation of *Taxi Driver*, for instance, expands on the script's world view, and screenwriter Robert Getchell took the unusual route of writing the novelisaton of his script of Martin Scorsese's *Alice Doesn't Live Here Anymore* (1974).

Stillman returned to the material, gauged it to the viewpoint of one of the film's characters, and provided an afterword in which the imaginary characters comment on what the real world made of their adventures. Stillman wrote the book from the perspective of Jimmy Steinway, the 'least important' and most apprehensive member of the group; like rewriting *Chinatown* from the perspective of Duffy, the assistant, or *Casablanca* from the viewpoint of Sascha, the bartender or Carl, the maitre d'.

In the chapter of retrospective reflection on the events of the book and movie, Stillman offers his own auto-critique of *The Last Days of Disco*, indeed of all of his films, concluding that it was a pretty accurate version of the 'real' events. The novel also ties several of the characters by relation or friendship to those in Stillman's other films, creating a mini-universe along similar lines to that created by Tarantino in his crime films.

The theme of *Disco*, stated broadly, is appearance versus reality, a theme as classic and old as Shakespeare. Nothing in the world of the discothèque is what it seems. Some patrons are really federal officers, the owners are really money launderers, seductive men happen to have venereal diseases, and Des pretends to be grappling with his sexuality in order to escape arguments with girlfriends. Only Josh and Alice are what they appear to be, and their qualities put them at odds with society, Josh for his fits of 'mania' and Alice for her self-undermining ways. This is where the dialogue about *Lady and the Tramp* comes into play. Much more than just a cultural allusion, the passage contains the moral point of the film. 'The only sympathetic character, the little Scotty who's concerned about Lady,' complains Josh, 'is mocked as old-fashioned and irrelevant, and shunted off to the side.' Josh is offering a pointed critique of Des, and warning Alice off of him, using the disguise of a cultural critique. Alice doesn't take the hint, but she never really likes Des as much as everyone thinks she does. All along, Alice likes Josh. As true to his conservative values as he is to happy endings, Stillman allows everything to work out well for the characters – even more so in the novelisation. Ultimately, it is better to be Josh than it is to be Des.

Like many independent writer-directors, such as the Coen Brothers, Stillman has drifted from original creations to adaptations. Although his potential adaptation of *Red Azalea*, as Stillman has reported in interviews, now appears to have collapsed, his work on Christopher Buckley's *Little Green Men*, at the time of writing, looks to be going ahead.

The problem for Stillman is surely to find books that reflect his philosophy, which he may have done with *Little Green Men*, a novel written by Christopher Buckley, the satirical novelist who is the son of conservative proselytiser William F Buckley. It is to be hoped that the more explicitly political work of Buckley will not tilt Stillman away from the expansive conservative vision that made his first three features a cohesive string of masterpieces.

# INDEPENDENT CINEMA AS TRULY INDEPENDENT: GUY MADDIN

There are some filmmakers who make both 'independent' and studio-financed features, such as Richard Linklater, Steven Soderbergh, Robert Rodriguez and Abel Ferrara, and there are others who are truly independent, and live, work and function wholly outside the system of commercial cinema, yet still manage to succeed. Jon Jost is an example, mentioned earlier. Jim Jarmusch is another. Also Hal Hartley, now, like Whit Stillman, relocated to France, and Melvin Van Peebles, who independently financed his film *Sweet Sweetback's Baadasssss Song* in 1971. And then there's Guy Maddin.

Canadian director Guy Maddin presents an interesting case, at least from the standpoint of a definition of independent film, because his evolution has been singular. To the outside observer, Maddin evolved from experimental filmmaker to art house favourite making feature films with notable performers. And, throughout his career, he has consistently financed his films independently, never directing television commercials or music videos for the cash or for career advancement.

His status as experimental filmmaker is slightly miscon-
strued, however. Based in Winnipeg, Maddin was an early
member of the influential but highly independent Winnipeg
Film Group. Like the group's other filmmakers, such as
John Paizs and Noam Gonick, Maddin was interested in
cinema from its roots: silent films and early sound films. In
his first films, Maddin was not so much 'experimenting'
with film in the manner of Stan Brakhage, but learning how
film worked by replicating, archly, the sort of old-fashioned
films he loved.

And though Canada has shown a vigorous attraction to
film production, thanks in large part to Thorold Dickinson
and the National Film Board of Canada, from which filmmakers such as Norman McLaren and Grant Munro
emerged, film funding is not as generous or as easy to
acquire as its competitive neighbours to the south tend to
believe. Maddin mostly financed his early films himself.

A typical Maddin project is an unpredictable blend of
silent cinema techniques, such as iris outs and title cards,
with tales of modern sexual anxiety. He tends to prefer
black and white images, studio sets (even for exteriors),
and actors who can replicate the hysteria of early silent
screen acting. His favoured settings are cultures and eras
that would normally be arcane to a child raised in North
America in the 1950s, such as Alpine villages and Russian
port cities. And Maddin's films can be confusing for some,
homages on the one hand to silent cinema, or perhaps a
campy trashing of it. Maddin tends to undercut the
dramatic tension of his tales with surrealistic images, odd
humour, and title cards that arrive as news bulletins, in

sentences that look undressed if they don't include exclamation points. In Maddin's intuitive approach to film, humour rides closely with tragedy, and highly serious moments can be presented as comedy, while comic moments can be executed with great solemnity.

Maddin was born in Winnipeg in 1956. His father was Charles Maddin, the manager of the hockey team the Winnipeg Maroons, and his mother, Herdis, helped run a hair salon with her family. The Maddins were of Icelandic heritage, and Maddin's subsequent films are filmed with lovingly mocking attitudes towards that tradition and its social signifiers.

Maddin was the youngest child in the family, his siblings all much older, and he has described his childhood as one spent mostly in front of that electronic babysitter, the television. His parents, already spent from raising the other kids, let Maddin roam free. As a child, Maddin had a fascination with both the beauty parlour and its various aromas, and its opposite, the smoke-filled and perspiration-scented hockey arena. Maddin came to find his family filled with tension, his father a typically overworked and withdrawn North American 1950s male. Despite that, Maddin grew to have an obsessive fear of his father's death, which eventually occurred in 1977.

After what appears to have been an indifferent school career, Maddin attended the University of Manitoba majoring in Business. He eventually dropped out and after working in a bank temporarily ended up a house painter.

While at University, however, Maddin fell in with a clutch

of friends who were fellow film buffs. They congregated at the home of film teacher Stephen Snyder. Maddin came to have a profound interest in the early days of cinema, perversely preferring the silent films of Eric von Stroheim, Lon Chaney, Carl Theodor Dreyer, and the Soviet Constructivists, among others, to contemporary cinema.

By 1986, Maddin was ready to make his first film. Predictably, perhaps, it expressed Maddin's anxiety and remorse about his father, but also explored the legacy of his father in Maddin himself. Called *The Dead Father* and long in the making, the film was financed by Maddin himself and he drew upon his friends, family, and the Winnipeg Film Group for help and support. Two years later he made *Tales from the Gimli Hospital*, a silent fantasia based loosely on an historical incident in which the Icelandic enclave in Gimli, Manitoba, was felled by a virus. In Maddin's hands, however, the event becomes a vehicle for his interests in obsessive love and male competition. For this film, Maddin received a Genie nomination for best screenplay.

Two years after *Gimli*, in 1990, Maddin released *Archangel*, a tale of amnesia and war set in the northern Russian port town of Archangel during the tail end of World War One. Even Maddin admits that the story was a little hard to follow, but it became a cult midnight movie hit and won the Best Experimental Film award from the National Society of Film Critics. *Archangel* marked Maddin's first collaboration with University of Winnipeg film professor George Toles, who would go on to write or co-write most of Maddin's subsequent features. Between feature films, Maddin continued to make anywhere from one to three short films, which would prove to be a solace when his career hit some rocky passages.

*Careful*, released in 1992, was Maddin's first colour film, and harks back to the silent Alpine film genre in which German director Leni Riefenstahl got her start. Deliberately provocative, the film covered a number of themes that were rising to the fore in Maddin's work, including incest, delirium and voyeurism, as it chronicled events in a mountain village where everyone must speak in whispers for fear of starting an avalanche. It was also the first film on which Maddin worked with a full crew, and part of the financing came from the Canadian government. *Careful* won the Best Canadian Film award at the Sudbury Cinefest, and has become the film best used to summarise what Maddin's work is all about. Though only 39, and with only three feature films to his credit, in 1995, Maddin received a life achievement award at the Telluride Film Festival.

A long filmmaking hiatus followed as Maddin's next big project, *The Dikemaster's Daughter*, fell through. Though he made several shorts, it took four years before Maddin attempted to shoot a feature. Unfortunately the result is a feature film that the director virtually disowns. *Twilight of the Ice Nymphs* (1997) may have a typically Maddin-sounding title, but was backed by a prominent Canadian film production company, and meant that Maddin did not have his usual level of control. Its typical indie cast included South African actress Alice Krige, Shelley Duvall and stand-up comic and impressionist Frank Gorshin. An hour-long documentary about Maddin's career, *Guy Maddin: Waiting for Twilight*, shot while he was making *Twilight*, charts his growing disenchantment and he announces his 'retirement' from filmmaking. *Twilight* was not a financial success.

Another long hiatus followed as Maddin evaluated his career. Then a summons came from the Toronto Film Festival to make a short film celebrating 100 years of cinema. Knowing that his fellow Canadian filmmakers, such as David Cronenberg and Atom Egoyan, would probably use long takes, Maddin decided to have as many edits in his film as humanly possible. The resulting short, *The Heart of the World*, was the real hit of the 2000 Toronto Film Festival, won six international awards including a Genie for Best Live Action Short Drama, and seems to have rejuvenated Maddin's career.

He went on to make an engaging record for the Canadian Broadcasting Corporation of the Royal Winnipeg Ballet's adaptation of Bram Stoker's 1897 novel, *Dracula*. Entitled *Dracula, Pages From a Virgin's Diary*, the film is both a grab bag of Maddin's visual and narrative wit, and an ecstatic account of the ballet. The film won an Emmy and two other awards. At the same time, Maddin was planning an unusual production, *Cowards Bend the Knee*, a distinctly autobiographical work but chopped up into ten parts and shown via separate peepholes as an art installation in a Toronto gallery. The film was eventually released in a more conventional manner in 2003. And 2003 turned out to be Maddin's *annus mirabilis*, as his most successful feature film, *The Saddest Music in the World*, came out, amid a wave of publicity and the garnering of six awards, including three Genies.

Since then, Maddin has made additional short films, including *My Dad is 100 Years Old* in collaboration with

Isabella Rossellini about her father, and another feature film (from an old but revised script), *Brand Upon the Brain!* (2006), shot in the United States. Maddin's most recent projects include a segment for the Brazilian omnibus film *Invisíveis, Os* made with five other directors, including Fernando E Solanas and Manoel de Oliveira, which is slated for release in 2008, and a documentary, *My Winnipeg*, which made its debut at the 2007 Toronto Film Festival.

### *Archangel* (1990)

**Directed by:** Guy Maddin
**Written by:** Guy Maddin, George Toles
**Produced by:** Greg Klymkiw
**Edited by:** Guy Maddin
**Cinematography:** Guy Maddin
**Cast:** Michael Gottli (Jannings), David Falkenburg (Geza), Michael O'Sullivan (Doctor), Margaret Anne MacLeod (Baba), Ari Cohen (Philbin), Sarah Neville (Danchuk), Kathy Marykuca (Veronkha), Kyle McCulloch (Lt John Boles)

In a complex plot that even the director admits can be confusing, Lt John Boles is a soldier missing a leg and suffering from amnesia, billeted in the Arctic port town of Archangel in Russia. World War One is now over, but, as the film announces, no one has bothered to tell the residents of Archangel. Nearby, the Russian Revolution is gaining speed. Boles mourns for his dead lover, Iris. He lives in the home of Veronkha and Philbin, her husband, who is also a soldier.

While Philbin has trouble remembering that he is married to Veronkha, Boles comes under the delusion that she is Iris. Meanwhile the war and revolution rages on.

If you have ever seen the horror film *White Zombie*, you have an idea of what Maddin is trying to achieve in his films. Released in 1932 and directed by Victor Halperin, the film stars Bela Lugosi as a voodoo master who makes a zombie out of the fiancée of a visiting gentleman, played by Robert Frazer. Indeed, Frazer would have made the perfect Maddin actor. Mourning what he thinks is the death of his fiancée, he becomes almost zombie-like himself with grief, alternately wandering around in a trance, weeping, drinking and visiting her grave to shed yet more tears over it. Though laughable today, Frazer's acting plays just in the key that appeals to Maddin, with male characters unleashing their broad, simple emotions (common to silent cinema) with no inhibitions.

*Archangel* is a virtual anthology of themes and images that would come to populate Maddin's subsequent films. Among them are amnesia, sexual competition between men, cowardice, the preparation of the human body as if it is a corpse, complex relations between parents and children, bizarre machinery and disastrous public performances. Most important are the skewed rules of conduct. Noting that the mother is whipping the child of the family John Boles is billeted with, Boles insists that he take over, since punishment of children is the job for a man (it doesn't occur to Boles that perhaps the punishment was unfair in the first place).

And of course there are the multiple allusions to early cinema, such as the name John Boles, taken from the actor and matinee idol whose career spanned roughly the years 1928 to 1938 (and also part of the name of a close friend). Maddin borrows imagery from Josef von Sternberg's *The Scarlet Empress* (1934) and elaborate costumery from the films of Eric von Stroheim. These elements are fully insinuated into the film and do not require the viewer's knowledge; Maddin's homage is both loving and campily parodic.

Archangel is arguably symbolic of Canada itself, a country forgotten, like Archangel, by the great world powers around it, who don't even take the city seriously enough to inform its inhabitants when the war is over. Canada's purported inferiority complex in comparison to the United States finds expression throughout Maddin's work, from the incestuous intermingling of citizens of the isolated Alpine village in *Careful*, to Chester Kent's pan-Americanism in *Saddest Music*. The multi-national casts that inhabit Maddin's films also suggest 'Canada'. The soldiers of Archangel are truly international; the dancer who plays Dracula in *Pages from a Virgin's Diary* is Asian; and the music contest in *Saddest Music* draws an international crowd to Winnipeg, reminiscent of the profound immigrant population of Canada.

Maddin's early films may at first seem 'primitive', but they contain beautiful imagery. Maddin has been heralded for his faithfulness to the look and feel of films from the 1920s, but the simultaneous mockery of the film even as it unspools suggests ambivalent feelings about the imagery. It is possible, after all, to love the cinema, and resent it for enslaving you. Maddin's comic tone is less a Brechtian distanciation than a disguise for the highly personal nature of most of the material in his films. From *The Dead Father* to *Saddest Music*, Maddin has been a confessional film-maker, but his offbeat humour and dramatic imagery deflect attention from him, even as he is the centre of his films.

### *The Heart of the World* (2000)

**Directed by:** Guy Maddin
**Written by:** Guy Maddin
**Produced by:** Jody Shapiro
**Edited by:** deco dawson, Guy Maddin
**Cinematography:** Guy Maddin
**Cast:** Leslie Bais (Anna), Caelum Vatnsdal (Osip), Shaun Balbar (Nikolai)

Two brothers love the same woman. The men are Nikolai, a mortician, and Osip, an actor currently playing Christ in a Passion play. The object of their competition is Anna, a 'top scientist'. She is unable to choose between the two siblings and instead opts for a rich industrialist, Akmatov. However, her choice may have caused a problem with the heart of the world, which resides at the earth's core and suffers a heart attack that threatens life on the earth. Anna kills Akmatov and slides down to the earth's core, sacrificing herself and saving the world by replacing the failed heart with her own. The world is then saved by the new message, Kino.

*Heart of the World* is highly characteristic of Maddin's prolific short film career. The music is dramatic, in this case Soviet composer Georgi Sviridov's energetic 'Time, Forward'. Shot in black and white, *Heart* is based on Soviet filmmaking models. It comprises a wealth of cuts, much more than average. Its narrative explores the sexual competition between two men for the same woman, only to lose her to a third, older, parental figure.

Snow, babies, organic matter, and other recurrent Maddin images all manage to make their presence felt. As the world is on the brink of doom, Maddin also manages to make the population of the earth act with the hysteria he demands of his actors.

As a celebration of cinema on its 100th birthday, *Heart of the World* is an exuberant collection of movie techniques that Maddin loves. While seeming like a parody, it is utterly consistent with his earlier personal films; all the more remarkable that Maddin is able to balance these different tones from film to film.

### *The Saddest Music in the World* (2003)

**Directed by:** Guy Maddin
**Written by:** Guy Maddin, George Toles, from a script by Kazuo Ishiguro
**Produced by:** Niv Fichman, Daniel Iron, Jody Shapiro
**Edited by:** David Wharnsby
**Cinematography:** Luc Montpellier
**Cast:** Mark McKinney (Chester Kent), Isabella Rossellini

(Lady Helen Port-Huntley), Maria de Medeiros (Narcissa), David Fox (Fyodor Kent), Ross McMillan (Roderick Kent/Gravillo the Great)

The setting is Winnipeg, during the Depression, in 1933. Beer magnate baroness Lady Helen Port-Huntley announces a contest, to find the saddest music in the world. Teams of musicians stream into Winnipeg, among them the Americanised former Winnipegan Chester Kent, a Broadway producer on the skids looking for one last payday. He is accompanied by his nymphomaniac, amnesiac girlfriend, Narcissa, who happens to be the spouse of Chester's brother, Roderick Kent, who mourns his dead son and his missing wife. Their father, an alcoholic doctor, once competed with Chester for the love of Lady Port-Huntley and is responsible for the loss of both her legs. Various reunions are compromised, and the contest, which comes down to Chester versus Roderick, ends with Lady Port-Huntley stabbing Chester with a shard of glass from her broken false legs. Roderick and Narcissa escape the burning contest hall while Chester remains behind amid the fire, playing the saddest music in the world, Narcissa's ballad.

*Saddest Music in the World* had all the hallmarks of another 'disaster' along the lines of *Twilight of the Ice Nymphs*: the film had a big novelty cast of professional international stars, including Isabella Rossellini, the daughter of Ingrid Bergman and Roberto Rossellini, Kids in the Hall member Mark McKinney, and Maria de Medeiros; financing from an outside source; and was an exotic tale of love and lust, of memory loss and intra-family sexual competition.

But somehow Maddin managed to make a success of it. His creative juices were flowing, he had a cast he was clearly comfortable with, and it was set explicitly in his own home town.

With a somewhat bigger budget, Maddin was able to experiment with the other facet of moviemaking that so fascinates him, sound production. From *Archangel* on, sound has been of utmost importance to the 'feel' of a Maddin film, and, as a musical, sound was going to be of particular importance in *Music.*

The film also manages to explore Maddin's ambivalent relationship with his country. Here, Winnipeg becomes a synecdoche of all Canada, as contestants from around the world (who surely spend as much money getting to the city as they might win in the competition itself), gather and impose an ethnic diversity on the city.

Maddin's films only get stronger as his career progresses. As a truly independent filmmaker he maintains the integrity of the art form while challenging its conventions and pushing it to new, always different heights.

## Interview with... Guy Maddin

How do you fund your films, broadly speaking? As I understand it, Canada has much more inclusive state grants than the United States (one more reason to move there?).

If a producer is lucky, he can get the state to cover half the budget with a loan, but not everyone is so lucky. For shorts and really low-budget affairs, Canada Council grants of up to $50,000 are awarded to a few applicants annually. I received a few of these over the years, but I don't think I've ever asked for the maximum amount. Our Manitoba Arts Council in my home province has been healthier than councils elsewhere in the country the last ten years, and that's made for a friendly filmmaking environment here in Winnipeg, but I try not to apply to it very often – I feel it's for artists either just starting out or those without any recourse to larger-budgeted affairs.

**Do you have a convenient definition of 'independent' cinema?**
Not a very good one. I feel independent, but I'm sure many people working for the man feel okay, too.

**Would you even call yourself an independent filmmaker? Or, if you have to have a label at all, would you call yourself something else: maverick, maudit, experimental?**
*Regie maudit* would be romantic. I don't know what an experimental filmmaker is – something to do with shooting blobs of paint floating on oil?

**Do you *want* money for films, or is there a certain dignity and purity in keeping the budgets low?**
Trying to raise money is time-consuming and humiliating. I'd rather shoot the precise moment I have just enough dough. That moment varies from project to project,

although I'm getting more and more impatient as I age and find myself happy to locate that moment sooner and sooner.

**According to the IMDB, *Saddest Music* cost $3.5 million Canadian. Is it terrifying to deal with such huge sums? Or is it peanuts, given that a movie such as *Narnia* costs $180 million?**
It still felt like peanuts, because it was.

**As your projects increase in complexity and expense, how do you manage to retain 'control' of a film? Or have you redefined for yourself the role of director?**
I have as much control as I want or I don't make the picture. I've enjoyed tackling assignments where my job is to please my boss, but I've always managed to serve my own purposes simultaneously. I've been lucky that way. The only project where I had little control was *Twilight of the Ice Nymphs*, where my producer broke his word to me and made unilateral decisions designed to serve himself. I was forced to shoot in 35mm when the script was a 16mm script and the production design was a 16mm production design and even the performances were 16mm. I was completely sucker-punched and had no idea how to get my footing back. He betrayed me at too many turns to count.

What are the differences in life on the set between mainstream movies, as you have experienced them in Winnipeg, and low-budget or indie films?

It's all very similar the world over I bet.

What changes in presentation or marketing, if any, do you anticipate with the advent of digitalised content and downloading capabilities on the Internet?

I embrace the future, believe it or not, but I am especially incapable of predicting it. Obviously big changes are afoot. As an old movie buff, I acknowledge that each change to cinema brought about by technological advances or social upheaval has been VERY EXCITING. I expect nothing less in the future.

# THE FUTURE OF INDEPENDENT CINEMA

In 1970, a minor actor and director named Tom Laughlin raised the financing for a feature film he wanted to make. He wrote it, starred in it, and cast his wife as the female lead. The character he played, Billy Jack, was the central figure in an earlier film Laughlin had made called *The Born Losers*, which he also wrote, directed, and starred in. The drive-in circuit success of that film helped Laughlin set up the more ambitious *Billy Jack*. Laughlin sold the finished film to Warner Bros, which released it in 1971. However, *Billy Jack* didn't do as well as Laughlin expected, and he successfully sued Warner Bros for the right to buy back the film from them. In 1973, Laughlin re-released *Billy Jack*, but this time distributing it himself via a system known at the time as 'four walling', in which distributors essentially rent the 'four walls' of a movie theatre for the run of a film's booking, keeping all the box office, while the theatre owner retains only the income from concessions. Four walling had been used before, but usually only for religious films or regional nature adventure tales such as *The Vanishing Wilderness*. Coupled with an aggressive television ad campaign, and a simultaneous national distribution of the film (called a wide release), *Billy Jack* went on to be a tremendous hit, making it for a time the most successful independent feature ever made. So successful was Laughlin's release pattern that the major studios mimicked it. *Jaws*, for example, benefited from a saturation ad campaign and wide release pattern in 1973, and the rest of the studios soon followed suit.

*Billy Jack*, essentially a martial arts film set amid the conflict between a hippie school and bigoted townspeople, is not anyone's contemporary idea of an independent feature. Still, it qualifies for the label thanks to its financing and distribution. In making the film, Laughlin went up against all three obstacles that usually stand in the way of a director wishing to enter the film business – financing, distribution, and advertising. Newcomers to the movie industry would tend to find it very difficult to raise the initial capital it takes to shoot a major motion picture. Only the studios have the finely honed knowledge of distribution patterns across the United States, indeed around the world. And they can afford the kind of saturation ad campaign that generally creates hits of even mediocre movies (or at least creates memorable impressions crucial for home viewing figures). Somehow Laughlin overcame all three impediments, and went on to write a book detailing his philosophy (*How to Invest in Motion Pictures... And Why You Shouldn't*, 1972).

The three basic elements of the film industry – production, distribution and exhibition – are designed to keep people out, as Martin Dale demonstrates in his book, *The Movie Game*. The amount of money necessary to buy a hand in that game is so prohibitive that ultimate control of the business rests with banks and the studios, which already have the infrastructure and connections necessary to finance, make and distribute films. As we have seen, distribution has been the bane of many a truly independent filmmaker since the advent of the sound era. A filmmaker's hopes often rest on the belief that if people can just get access to their movie, it will entertain or inform them and make enough money to pay the cast and crew.

In late 2006, David Lynch attempted to circumvent studio indifference to his recent films and the logjam of distribution by marketing directly to his fans. According to a report by Jeff Jensen in the 8 December 2006 *Entertainment Weekly*, Lynch took his most recent film, the epic-length, shot-on-video fantasia *Inland Empire*, starring Laura Dern and partially photographed in Poland, and attempted to distribute it himself. In addition, Lynch uses his titular website (www.davidlynch.com) to market artifacts from his various enterprises, which, to date, include DVDs of *Eraserhead*, mobile phone ring tones, computer screen 'wallpaper', and his own brand of coffee.

As of this writing, there are more 'independent' film distributors than ever, but fewer truly independent films. Each of the major distributors has an indie branch: Fox has Searchlight, Universal has Focus Features, Warner has Warner Independent and Picturehouse (a merger of Time Warner-AOL's Fine Line with the distribution arm of Newmarket), Sony has Sony Pictures Classics, Disney still has Miramax (though the Weinstein brothers have left), and Paramount has Vantage.

But now that the majors have their claws in the body

independent, its definition has changed yet again. Since there can be no economic classification of an independent film, it has evolved into a genre, with carefully cultivated audience expectations about the general nature of the 'product'. A perfect example would be *Little Miss Sunshine*, which was released by Fox Searchlight in 2006. It's a film that bears many of the attributes of the independent film as we have come to know it, and, as a reward, went on to make over $90 million and win two Oscars. Independent distributors still exist (they include Lions Gate Films, the company founded years ago by Robert Altman IFC Films, Samuel Goldwyn Films, The Weinstein Company and its horror film arm, Dimension Films, Magnolia Pictures, Palm Pictures, Tartan Films, ThinkFilm, and even George Lucas's Lucasfilm, which exists solely to make *Star Wars* movies), but they function in a circumscribed world thanks to the majors muscling in on their turf.

On the other hand, even today, ambitious filmmakers can manage to make a film and get people to see it. In 1997, Lance Weiler and Stefan Avalos made a movie for $900 called *The Last Broadcast*. It was based on their script, but also partly improvised. *The Last Broadcast* tells the story of a reporter looking into some mysterious deaths. A few years earlier two cable access TV show hosts, their cameraman and a 'psychic', travelled to the Pine Barrens of southern New Jersey in search of the so-called Jersey Devil, a mythical figure akin to the Yeti or Bigfoot. There, while isolated in the woods, most of the party was killed, with the psychic later being accused of the crimes. The reporter David Leigh (David Beard) incorporates 'found' footage that the cable hosts shot for their own film into an assembly that makes a reasonably coherent account of their fate. The reporter also incorporates his own, new footage, some of which is of him addressing the camera, but also includes 'neutral' footage that reveals the surprise ending.

If the plot of *The Last Broadcast* sounds vaguely familiar it is because its process and realisation mirrors that of *The Blair Witch Project* (1999). Written and directed by two Florida-based filmmakers, Daniel Myrick and Eduardo Sánchez, *Blair Witch* became a sensation, in part because of the innovative and ambiguous ad campaign of its distributor, Artisan, which exploited the Internet and kept it unclear whether the film was real or fictional.

Though *The Blair Witch Project* may resemble *The Last Broadcast* in theme and style, the two films diverged in other respects. *Blair Witch* was conventionally distributed, on film, to nationwide theatres. *The Last Broadcast* was distributed via satellite, using then-progressive technology to escape the dauntingly high costs of making individual prints. (It's worth noting that both films resemble the much earlier *Cannibal Holocaust* from 1980.) It has only been in the last few years that movie theatres have adopted some of the innovations that brought *The Last Broadcast* to individual screens as a digitally projected image. Is it too late? Just as newspapers are fretting publicly about dying in the face of digital competition, so movie theatre chains are concerned about shifts in cinema-going habits.

Today there is much more competition for the consumer

dollar than there was, say, in 1951, the year of the last great crisis in Hollywood, the so-called Consent Decree, the result of an anti-trust suit that severed the studios from the theatres they owned in an intricate, market-dominating form of vertical integration. Combined with the rise of tele-vision, this blow to the movies resulted in the creation or exploitation of 3-D, CinemaScope and other widescreen processes. But back then, it was *only* television and radio that distracted the audience's attention. Television was piped free into most people's homes, and the public seemed to settle for the small, unstable, black and white image, as well as the simplicity of network programming, modelled, for the most part, on radio.

Today, audiences are subdivided by analysts according to age, ethnicity, sex and income, amongst other markers, and never before have movie audiences been so segmented. Take the 13 to 18 male age group, so coveted by movie studios; its members are easily distracted by television, sports events, comic books, the world wide web, portable gaming devices, Blackberries and other text messaging devices, and videogames, an industry with annual revenues of around $7 billion.

One method adopted in certain markets to spark movie attendance is a return to elegance in the movie place. One of the main complaints of most moviegoers is that the *other* audience members are loud and disruptive. Only secondarily do they complain about bad projection, which is rife among theatre chains whose individual venues are operated by teenagers under modest supervision, or the wares on sale at the concession stand, usually prefab boxed candy and overpriced popcorn. There are reasons why the average theatre has sunk into a lawless zone. Fear of litigation often prevents theatre managers from acting decisively against disruptive patrons, and the mark-up on concessions is vast, providing most of that cinema's revenue. The Arc Light in Los Angeles and the Cinetopia Theater in Vancouver, Washington are just two examples of cinemas that offer a return to order and cleanliness. The cost of the tickets may be higher, but the viewer is assured expert projection, with Cinetopia adding the innovation of projecting digital images that are indistinguishable from traditional film images.

Movies, as the public have come to know them for over 100 years, are on the verge of radical change. Since the late 1970s at least, with the introduction of home video, an implacable force of change has been on the march. Home entertainment centres, iPods, Bittorrent trading, and the world wide web itself are just a few of the mutations that have revolutionised how we view movies and how we find out about them. One of the most vivid shifts among so many is that a movie, as we customarily know it, may cease to be a physical thing. Taking a page, as it were, out of the aesthetics of Monroe Beardsley, who argued that a work of art is a perceptual object rather than a physical one, movies are now more often than not a digital object.

Predictions of the eventual digital hosting, projection, copying, and so forth, of movies have been rampant since the early 1990s, or at least since the inception of *Wired* magazine. In early December 2006, a step toward modernity was taken when the six-screen Living Room Theaters complex opened in downtown Portland, Oregon. Offering a complete leisure experience, the theatre has a restaurant, a bar, free wi-fi, and six small auditoria (the largest has 65 seats). The company putting the project together has a sister theatre in Miami. What is most unusual about Living Room Theaters is that the founders also plan to exclusively screen independent and 'specialty' (that is, foreign) films, often trafficking in films that have not yet premiered in the United States, and in some cases dealing directly with the filmmakers, circumventing the lugubrious, arcane, and outsider-excluding mechanics of national distribution, the stumbling block that fells most bright ideas in film produc-tion and exhibition.

The brainchild of Felix Martin, Ernesto Rimoch and Diego Rimoch, Living Room Theaters is at the very least an ambi-tious enterprise that prides itself on its energy conservation and green policies, and it aspires to tear customers away from the mundane reliance on popcorn, candy and soda pop as inevitable movie-time concessions. Shawn Levy of the *Oregonian*, who covered the theatre's creation exten-sively, wrote that, 'Martin and his partners currently operate a firm which converts celluloid prints of movies into digital files that can be projected in movie houses, and they are establishing connections with independent and foreign film-makers who don't have distribution in the United States'.

It's a curious coincidence that only a year earlier Cinetopia, another digital theatre with eight screens, a full restaurant, and 'gourmet' butter for popcorn, went up in Vancouver, Washington, just across the river from Portland. Cinetopia appears to have made itself a rousing success by showing a mix of popular hits, such as *Casino Royale*, along with the studios' definition of art films, such as *Babel*, as well as digital projection of football games on Sunday and Monday. By coincidence, Cinetopia calls its three fine-dining theatres, where waiters serve spectators candy, pop, beer/wine, and/or hot meals prior to curtain, Living Room Theaters. The presence of these two venues within 15 miles of each other suggests that Portland and its environs are plugged unwittingly into the zeitgeist.

One wonders if the earnest founders of Living Room Theaters know what they are getting into. From the local arena to the national they may be greeted with resistance or, worse, indifference. Circumvented distributors may not be so happy about offering up, at good terms, the films that Living Room Theaters want to book. Film fanatics may decide that it is still cheaper to stay home with their own television – equivalent these days to a cinema presentation – than to venture out. And finally there is the issue of where Living Room Theaters resides, which happens to be a busy but recently gentrified section of the city called the Pearl District, for reasons no one seems to remember. The residents mostly consist of very wealthy but conventional people living in high-rise condos, likely to be frustrated that the local cinema is showing the latest Argentine intellectual thriller rather than *Superman Returns*. Worse, the company's founders may have overestimated the town's general appetite for off-beat entertainment, although the theatre complex's presentation as a multi-faceted 'experience' seems to indicate an awareness of this possibility.

Worst of all, Portland filmgoers have long been dominated by one large solo theatre chain or another, all of which have flirted with federal anti-trust suits. Currently, it is Regal Cinemas that owns most of the city's screens. Outside of the Regal chain, there are a handful of independent theatres scattered around the city that show either second run, revival, or repertory calendars, among them the Cinema 21 and the Hollywood Theater. The near-monopoly that rules first-run Portland theatre-going has been aggressive in the past about preserving its hegemony, regardless of who the nominal CEO happens to be.

So, the existence of Living Room Theaters currently looks good for Portland viewers, but what are the international implications? Moving image technology may advance and improve, but people don't change and new technology tends to appeal to our inherent laziness. Ultimately, success in exhibition originates with what the film industry likes to call product. If Living Room Theaters can triumph over inertia and audiences attend their cinemas in high numbers, theirs may be the model that other theatres and other countries follow.

Changes in market forces that occur as studios battle it out with one another, and different formats go head to head, will also determine the future of independent cinema.

James Schamus, for example, is worried. Currently the head of Focus Features, Schamus also laboured in the indie trenches, as a screenwriter and producer. In collaboration with Ang Lee, he produced *The Ice Storm* (1997), *Ride with the Devil* (1999), *Hulk* (2003), *Brokeback Mountain* (2005) and *Lust, Caution* (2007). Now he is an executive, able to 'green light' projects.

But at the 2006 Independent Spirit Awards, Schamus let loose in his keynote address on the state of independent filmmaking. His remarks were later published in the winter 2006 issue of *Filmmaker* magazine. Schamus began by suggesting, tongue-in-cheek, that the Independent Feature Project, which sponsors the awards, and the Spirit Awards themselves, be disbanded.

'The war is over,' he declared, 'and we should all now happily celebrate around the pyre of our victory bonfire the accomplishments that have brought the independent movement this far, and wonder, perhaps, if from the ashes something new might arise.'

Schamus then shared some startling statistics. In 1986, at the first Spirit Awards, the total box office of the nominated films in all categories was about $20 million. Fifteen years later, the total box office for all nominated films was $300 million, indicating an exponential rise in the 'economic heft' of independent films.

'The films recognised at the Spirit Awards,' Schamus declared, 'have succeeded overwhelmingly in entering the mainstream system of commercial exploitation and finance, and today the economics required to make oneself heard even as an 'independent' are essentially studio economics.'

But as Schamus made clear, he was worried 'not so much about "independent film" as about independence itself – the preservation of some form of civic space in which freedom of expression is not merely a privilege purchased with the promise of an eventual profit, but the exercise of a fundamental right.' Schamus then listed threats to independent cinema, indeed all cinema. First there is 'the immensity of the consolidation of market share and political power that has occurred in the media industries during the Clinton Administration,' which, in his view, threatens, 'freedom of expression, diversity of opinion, and open access to markets and audiences that the astonishing growth of the horizontally integrated media giants portends'. Second is the '1996 Telecommunications Act, which has led to one of the greatest boondoggles in American history (the giveaway of over $15 billion in broadcasting spectrum) and which is one of the most important factors in the increasing consolidation of the American and global media worlds, and a new mandate for aggressive anti-trust enforcement'.

Finally, Schamus lists 'the World Trade Organization (WTO) and the World Intellectual Property Organization's (WIPO) intellectual property talks,' which 'support the existence of what's left of independent media companies overseas. American independent cinema has long depended on far-thinking foreign distributors and public television stations for much of its economic sustenance. With the Hollywood majors now grabbing an average of between 75 and 90% of the box office of most foreign territories, and with huge transnational satellite and cable TV companies wiping out local TV competition, the number of buyers, especially those with access to lucrative pay-TV deals, is shrinking'.

Are there any clues in the history of cinema as to what might happen in our current and future climate? Technology is as different as it has ever been, though processing content that is the same as always. The work of independent filmmakers grouped under the label Mumblecore, and independents such as Lance Weiler and Bilge Ebiri, might usefully suggest different avenues of both content and exhibition.

The core of Mumblecore are Andrew Bujalski (*Funny Ha Ha* [2002] and *Mutual Appreciation* [2006]), Joe Swanberg (*Kissing on the Mouth* [2005] and *Hannah Takes the Stairs* [2007]) and Jay Duplass (*The Puffy Chair* [2005]). The films themselves share common themes and production styles, such as micro budgets, non-professional actors, and tales about the difficulties of romantic relationships among people in their 20s. There are also subtle differences. Bujalski's films appear improvised, but are in fact carefully scripted, like those of the major Mumblecore influence, John Cassavetes. The Chicago-based Swanberg does allow improvisation, and his films are notable for their explicit sex scenes. Swanberg is also an advocate of Internet-based distribution for his films.

Weiler's *The Last Broadcast* seemed to be the techno wave of movie exhibition's future; though there's always someone in the movie business who predicts that satellite broadcasts will soon supersede celluloid, it hasn't yet come to pass, partly because DVDs and digital home download have edged it out. His latest film, the evocative horror film, *Head Trauma*, which he directed, shot and edited alone, shows the range of accomplishments that a contemporary filmmaker can achieve outside the Hollywood system. Those familiar with *The Last Broadcast* will see similar themes: mysterious figures in the forest, interpersonal incompetence, hubris, and an unexpected narrative twist.

*Head Trauma* tells the story of one George Walker (Vince Mola, a sort of Francis Ford Coppola clone). After living on the road or on the streets for some 20 years, he returns to the home of his late grandmother, a building that is now a condemned structure in a lower-middle-class neighbourhood. With the help of Julian (Jamil AC Mangan), the African-American youth next door, who is also a gifted cartoonist, George attempts to clean up the house and rescind the condemnation, in the face of obstacles from an old high-school rival who stands to profit from its destruction. Also impeding George's labours are the bad dreams he has, in which mysterious images rattle around in his head, among them a small feminine figure whose features are obscured by a large hood (like the running figure in *Don't Look Now*), and some disturbing activity in a wooded field.

*Head Trauma* is a psychological thriller of precision and insight. George is not a particularly sympathetic character, it soon turns out, and he tends to destroy potential relationships before they even happen, especially with an old flame from the neighbourhood, Mary (Mary Monahan). He doesn't need his old rival to sabotage his house. George is fully capable of sabotaging it himself.

Although at first it seems like *Head Trauma* is going to be an 'old dark house' horror film, it plays in the tradition of thrillers that include *An Occurrence at Owl Creek Bridge, Jacob's Ladder* and *Angel Heart*, with some of its suspense created by unseen antagonists, and psychological tension in the mould of Roman Polanski and Nicolas Roeg. Weiler has a knack for making empty rooms in daylight and the woods in the afternoon feel decidedly ominous.

Weiler's script is lean and mean; and there is no subplot to speak of. The film is creepy, with the added help of excellent music and sound production. It looks good for a film shot on HD video: very controlled and precise. There are even superb aerial shots. Weiler was able to achieve all this on a budget of only $126,000.

Another example of the tenacity of independent film-makers is found in the career of Bilge Ebiri. A Turkish-American filmmaker who is also a journalist, Ebiri was born in 1973 in England, and ended up at Yale, where his thesis film, *Bad Neighborhood*, won the Lamar Prize. He worked on films by Russian director Nikita Mikhalkov, Brett Parker and Daniel Adams, and eventually became a film critic for *New York* magazine and Nerve.com. His first feature film, a thriller in the Heroic Alienation mode, *New Guy*, was released in 2004.

*New Guy* tells the story of the new employee, Gregg (Kelly Miller), who, on his first day of work in a large corpo-rate office, finds the environment increasingly strange. When he is accidentally locked into the building at closing time, he discovers its real secrets. *New Guy* is an efficient comic thriller, and follows at least one indie-filmmaking pattern in being shot in one basic location.

It's a story inflected with strains of Russian literature, in which the normal world is 'made strange'. The odd things he sees in the building, such as men weeping inexplicably, continually confound Gregg. In one regard, the narrative is an allegory for the immigrant experience, with a stranger to the ways of the corporation trying to fit in while feeling at odds with the physical surroundings and the codes of behaviour.

It's not easy to make a movie, any movie, but Ebiri has shot one, with a budget of about $55,000, $30,000 of it coming from his own savings, is writing another 'microbudget' film, and is directing a 'six-figure' budget film in Turkey. From his command centre in Brooklyn, New York, he has managed to gather the resources to make one well-received feature film and use it as a platform for further work. It hasn't been easy, but filmmaking rarely is.

# INTERVIEWS WITH...

## Lance Weiler

**It seems to me that the movie industry has been a little short sighted in not taking up the technological break-throughs you established with your first film, *The Last Broadcast*. Did you find it hard to capitalise on its success to advance to the 'next step' of your career, so to speak?**
In some respects, yes, and others, no. In a lot of ways we were ahead of the curve with how we made and distributed *The Last Broadcast*. So we found ourselves at a strange place. On the one hand, people respected what we'd done, on the other they had no clue. Sometimes people get hung up on aspects of the work. For instance they'd say, '*The Last Broadcast* – that's a nice documentary but can you do narrative?' They miss the point. Sometimes the technical aspects got in the way of the story but I think there's always some form of struggle to get the work made and to get it seen.

**What was the genesis of *Head Trauma*?**
*Head Trauma* comes out of two life experiences that took me to very dark places The first was a head-on collision

with a garbage truck that almost killed me. Twelve years ago I was lying in a hospital bed with a severe head injury and my jaw wired shut. I could have died that day; stupidly I wasn't wearing my seat belt – my jaw snapped the steering wheel and my head busted the windshield and thankfully I lost consciousness. After the accident I was plagued by vivid nightmares of the crash until one day they just stopped.

Flash forward to 2000 and I'm pitching a TV show to some major networks. After a year of pitching we land at a network and after a roller coaster ride that takes another two years of the show being on again, off again, we received money to shoot a pilot. Working on the show ranks as one of the worst professional experiences I've had. At times it really felt like I was a tenant farmer not a co-creator executive of a major network show. In the end we shot a great pilot but it died a slow, painful death and I felt like I went through the five stages of grief. So in the winter of 2003, when I was feeling like shit and unsure of what to do, a few simple words changed my path. I owe huge thanks to my wife Jennifer for simply saying, 'Do what you love, just make another movie'. It's so obvious but at the time I was out of my head. And that's the series of events that created *Head Trauma*.

**Why make a 'horror' film? Why that genre? What does horror offer you or inspire in you that you can't get elsewhere?**

I love the horror genre. There is something interesting to me about exorcising those demons, those dark things that rest in one's mind – it's a way to get them out of your own head and do something productive with them. I've had some dark times in my life. When I was younger I almost drowned and at the age of 14 my house burned down, and then the car accident. I always like to have some autobiographical element within my films. Water and fire play an important role within *Head Trauma,* as does the concept of a blow to the head.

**Given that it is a lot easier to make movies these days, what remains the most difficult aspect of filmmaking?**
By far the most difficult aspect of filmmaking these days isn't a production issue it's promotion-distribution. With over 20,000 feature films being made due to the boom in digital production the chances of a film being seen beyond a film festival are rare. Releasing a truly independent film into today's market without millions for P&A [print and advertising] can be very difficult. But thanks to the web there are ways to build an audience and get the word out in very effective ways. For instance the web comic for *Head Trauma* is not a normal film site (<http://headtraumamovie.com>) – it is an interactive comic with some twisted stuff hidden under the surface. It becomes an extension of the story. Now more than ever it is important to create extra value for the fans. With *Head Trauma* I'm working hard to give a good presentation from start to finish. I've been on the other end and I know what type of things hook me in. That is really the issue – knowing your audience and then finding a way to get the work to them.

**Can you talk about the subject of your next feature film?**
Yeah, it's a really dark and twisted flick set in the remote wilderness. It's based on an actual experience of my life that occurred while I hiked a part of the Appalachian Trail called the 'Wilderness'. The AT is a wild place and being alone for 10 to 12 days with no civilisation in sight can be very creepy.

## Interview with Bilge Ebiri

**It seems as if an 'independent' filmmaker has to do everything: write, edit, shoot, score sometimes, and even raise money. Is this burdensome or exciting?**
I am of the firm belief that, while a filmmaker should exert as much control as possible over his/her film, they should not do everything. I suppose there may be a filmmaker out there who happens to be an incredible screenwriter, incredible director, incredible cinematographer, incredible editor, incredible composer, and incredible fund-raiser all at once. But I haven't come across that person yet. (I always thought John Carpenter was a terrible composer, for example. And I'm not particularly keen on Vincent Gallo as an editor.)

I personally like the process of collaboration on screenplays. And I insist on working with an editor. In fact, I encourage other filmmakers to work with an outside editor, and I also believe that an editor shouldn't be present on the set of the film. You *need* that second set of eyes to go over your footage, to see it without the prejudices created by the ordeal of your shoot. On *New Guy* there were shots and scenes that had been atrociously difficult to get – footage that had taken us hours and hours of shooting late into the night, with many problems, that I was finding very hard to let go in the editing room. Had it not been for my editor, Cabot Philbrick's, fresh set of eyes, and his willingness to give me the unvarnished truth at all times, I think the result would have been a lesser film.

You need that extra set of eyes, because – no big surprise here – a film as originally conceived is more often than not very different from the film that winds up getting made. Godard has that great quote about how when he made *Breathless* he thought he was making *Scarface* and wound up making *Alice in Wonderland*. I guess we're lucky that he had the clarity of vision to realise that, but I suspect many filmmakers out there wouldn't have been able to. Imagine what we might have lost if *Breathless* had remained an unconsciously misbegotten genre flick rather than something new.

That said, the reason many independent filmmakers wind up doing everything is simple: cost. It's cheaper to score your own movie. Same with editing, and so on. It's hard to argue with that. But I have always felt that it's important to get the best people available for the resources you have. Are you the best composer for the resources you have? You can get the rights to recordings of Mozart, Beethoven, Bach, Handel, Prokofiev, et al for a couple of hundred bucks a pop. I used classical pieces by Holst and De Falla in *New Guy*. It cost me a lot less than if I were to book studio and recording time and order pizzas for my friend's band.

**Do you think your movies would be 'better' if you had more money? Or do you subscribe to the 'low budgets make you think harder' ethos?**

Well, low budgets definitely make you think harder. But there are thresholds. I mean, it takes a certain amount of money to produce a film. You can reduce the amount, but at some point you wind up making sacrifices you don't want to make. The most important thing you lose is time. We had 17 days of shooting scheduled for *New Guy*, and two of them were half-days. We wound up needing 19 total (still with the two half-days, so it probably added up to more like 18). If I hadn't had those extra two days, I would quite simply not have had a movie. And if I had had two more, I guarantee you I would have had a better movie.

That said, I'm not of the belief that more money means better movies. You need the money that gives you the freedom you need (not necessarily the freedom you want), and the minimum of technical competence (clear sound, decent stock, an electrical outlet, etc) to get something on film (or video) that will result in something someone else will want to watch.

There's another issue here, which is style. Because of the kinds of directors I like and the kinds of films that influenced me, I prefer a more elegant style – fluid camera moves, more classical composition and lighting – to a really gritty, handheld style. These things cost more money. Dolly tracks cost money. Steadicams cost an unholy shitload of money. Grips – or at least grips with steady hands – cost money. Similarly, non-professional or inexperienced actors are fine depending on the kind of film you're making.

Vittorio de Sica got away with non-professionals. But Ingmar Bergman probably couldn't. So, while I'm often very impressed by a guy like Joe Swanberg shooting these very impersonal, semi-improvised films on a dime, I also know that it's probably not part of my cinematic DNA. But who knows?

**Is there a particular stage of the filmmaking process that you like the best?**
I hate writing, for the most part. But I think on some level you have to hate writing. Writing shouldn't come easy. If it's easy you're doing something wrong. Similarly, a producer friend of mine once said that every troubled shoot she'd been on had resulted in a successful film – and the more troubled, the more successful. She was saying this to me during one of the darker days of the *New Guy* shoot.

I do like shooting and editing. Shooting is great because you're finally seeing things play out, and knocking them off the list. There's a real sense of progress. It's exciting. Editing is also great (especially if you're working with a good editor) because you're finally seeing scenes come together, trying things out.

I have to say, another part of the process I really enjoy is auditioning actors. I never auditioned actors until *New Guy*, and I thought I was going to hate it, that it was going to be a tedious slog, that everybody was going to be terrible. But it was actually really exciting – people came in and brought new things to the material, to the parts. It was electrifying, in a way. If they were bad it was entertaining. If they were good it was really entertaining. I could let my imagination run away with thinking of different people in different parts. I also did a couple of auditions where I just had people improvise scenes. I loved it. I can't wait to do it again.

### Do you become a 'different person' while directing?

Yes. I wish I could become more of a different person, though. But because I tend to work with friends this makes it a bit harder. I would love to arrive on set, not know anybody, have them not know who I am, then assume the role of the all-powerful, sadistic director, then leave with the footage and edit it somewhere else. But that's not going to happen.

Basically, I can be a shy person in my ordinary life, but a director simply can't be shy. If you're shy on set, then you're not a director. You're a PA for your cameraman. But I do become more focused, more direct, more outspoken, more energetic.

### Movies tend to be so expensive: how do you find the financing?

It has always seemed to me to be absurd that people – often complete strangers – give loads of money to people to produce low-budget indie films, which almost as a rule don't make money. I made *New Guy* mostly with money I had saved up from three years of working three jobs. I knew a number of people who had scripts they wanted to produce, and who then went off to look for money, and then got stuck at that stage of the process. I was determined to not let that happen. So I had no retirement savings, I worked several jobs, saved up, didn't spend anything on anything, knowing that I was going to need the money to make a film. I didn't want to be the guy who spent ten years looking for money for a small film that itself wasn't going to make any money.

For my next film I am actually working with people who have more experience in producing and raising money, so I will hopefully have a better answer for you in a couple of years. When you interview me in debtors' prison.

**As a critic yourself, do you have a different perspective about reviews of your work?**

Before I premiered *New Guy*, I actually sat down and composed a really negative review of it – the most damning review that film has ever received, trust me – just to prepare myself for the onslaught of condemnation the film was certain to receive. (Then I deleted it, just to make sure I wouldn't dwell on it.) But, lo and behold, the reviews were good. The *Variety* review was good. The audience response was, by and large, positive. And when it was released in New York I got good reviews from the *Times*, from *Time Out*. Even the mixed or negative reviews – the *Village Voice*, the *NY Post* – weren't so bad. I have had a couple of dismissive, truly negative reviews, but they didn't bother me. Honestly, if I was a critic and had to review *New Guy*, I don't know what I would say.

**Is film 'film' anymore? Do you have nostalgia for the big-screen world of movies? Or do you find that TV, straight to video, and online broadcasting offer potential?**

Well, the other formats offer potential, but obviously movie theatres have their place. I'm not nostalgic about it, though, because that world still exists. I don't think the big-screen world of movies will disappear. The things that disappear are the things that inconvenience people. Movie theatres, as far as I can tell, are not yet an inconvenience. Not everyone wants to sit at home and watch films with the whole family. It may become increasingly difficult for a certain kind of independent film to get theatrical distribution. But just as the prices of flat-screen HDTVs are falling, so too are the prices of digital projection equipment. It's possible that 10–20 years from now we'll be looking on our current period as the beginning of the micro cinema movement.

**At what point does one 'feel' like a real filmmaker?**
It has nothing to do with the filmography and everything to do with how you feel about yourself. I've got a number of films in my filmography, and I've made money as a filmmaker, and yet I still have trouble calling myself a filmmaker, because I make most of my money as a film critic, and that's how most people in my professional circle know me. But I know people who call themselves filmmakers even though they haven't released a single film yet. I know people who have been working on their first film for the past five years. Should that person not call themselves a filmmaker? They go to a production office or an editing room every day to make a film. They are filmmakers.

Indeed, sometimes it takes that psychological shift – to stop dreaming of the day when you're going to be a filmmaker and to start calling yourself one – to actually get the motivation going. In early 2001, I woke up one morning, after having a particularly miserable couple of months, and said, 'Fuck this. It's time to make the first one'. I told everyone I knew that I was going to make a feature film – just so that I would be held to it, so that I couldn't weasel my way out of it. By June 2002, the cameras were rolling. By March 2003, I was premiering it in California. And by the end of 2003, I had taken it around the world. And by the end of 2004, it had a theatrical release.

## Has anything about your filmmaking experience surprised you?

I had worked on lots of movie sets, so the process had already been demystified for me by the time I started to make my own films. I already knew that it was a physical ordeal, that the sight of a bunch of guys in overalls, with their ass-cracks showing, hauling cable is a lot closer to the actual experience of filmmaking than a bunch of film nerds arguing over whether Tsai Ming Liang has 'finally lost it' outside of Alice Tully Hall (though that certainly has its place, too).

But I guess the thing I learned from my own process, and which I tell everyone is: the things that you don't worry about are the things that will go wrong. The things that you do worry about are, by and large, the things that go fine. I worried about location, and actors, and sound. I had an amazing location, amazing actors, and amazing sound. I didn't worry about extras. I didn't worry about people arriving on time at the set. I didn't worry about not having enough PAs. You can imagine the rest.

But there's no mystery to that, either. The lesson there is simply that you have to worry about everything. Then you'll be fine.

# INDEPENDENT FILM RESOURCES

## DVD

Most modern independent films are available on DVD, primarily because they are recent. The further back in time the film was made, the less likely it is to be available on DVD or VHS. Kenneth Anger's films are beginning to come out on DVD (from Fantomas), for example, as are a selection of films by Stan Brakhage (Criterion). The films of Maya Deren are available (from Zeitgeist) as is *Salt of the Earth* (Alpha).

The five directors treated in this book are well represented on DVD. Jill and Karen Sprecher's *Clockwatchers* (Sundance) is out of print, while *Thirteen Conversations About One Thing* (Sony Pictures Classics) is available. Of James Mangold's films, *Heavy* (Sony), *Cop Land* (Miramax), *Girl, Interrupted* (Columbia), *Kate and Leopold* (Miramax), *Identity* (Columbia), and *Walk the Line* (Fox) are all available on DVD. Of Whit Stillman's films, *Metropolitan* (Criterion) and *Barcelona* (Warner) are available while *The Last Days of Disco* (Polygram) is out of print. Guy Maddin's feature films are all available on DVD: *Careful* (Kino), *Archangel* with *The Heart of the World* (Zeitgeist) and *The Saddest Music in the*

*World* (MGM). Criterion has issued a box set featuring five of John Cassavetes's films. Bilge Ebiri's *New Guy* (Vanguard) and Lance Weiler's *The Last Broadcast* (Wavelength) and *Head Trauma* (Heretic) are available.

## Books

The following books on various aspects of independent cinema were consulted in the writing of this Kamera Book and are highly recommended.

Allen, Michael, *Contemporary U.S. Cinema*, Pearson Education, 2003

Andrew, Geoff, *Stranger Than Paradise: Maverick Film-Makers in Recent American Cinema*, Limelight Editions, 1999

Arthur, Paul, *A Line of Sight: American Avant-Garde Film Since 1965*, University of Minnesota Press, 2005

Balio, Tino, *The American Film Industry*, University of Wisconsin Press, 1976

Bernardoni, James, *The New Hollywood*, McFarland, 1991

Biberman, Herbert, *Salt of the Earth: The Story of a Film*, Harbor Electronic Publishing, 2003

Biskind, Peter, *Down and Dirty Pictures: Miramax, Sundance, and the Rise of Independent Film*, Simon and Schuster, 2004

Bordwell, David, *The Way Hollywood Tells It*, University of California Press, 2006

Braddock, Jeremy & Hock, Stephen, *Directed By Allen Smithee*, University of Minnesota Press, 2001

Brown, Gene, *Movie Time: A Chronology of Hollywood and the Movie Business from its Beginnings to the Present*, Macmillan, 1995

Butsch, Richard, *The Making of American Audiences: From Stage to Television, 1750–1990*, Cambridge University Press, 1999

Carney, Ray, *Cassavetes On Cassavetes*, Faber and Faber, 2001

Carson, Diane, *John Sayles: Interviews*, University of Mississippi Press, 1999

Crabb, Kelly Charles, *The Movie Business: The Definitive Guide To The Legal And Financial Secrets Of Getting Your Movie Made*, Simon and Schuster, 2005

Dale, Martin, *The Movie Game: The Film Business In Britain, Europe, and America*, Cassell, 1997

Dixon, Wheeler Winston, *The Second Century of Cinema: The Past and Future of the Moving Image*, State University of New York Press, 2000

Epstein, Edward Jay, *The Big Picture: The New Logic Of Money And Power In Hollywood*, Random House, 2005

Fine, Marshall, *Accidental Genius: How John Cassavetes Invented the American Independent Film*, Miramax Books, 2005

Finler, Joel W, *The Hollywood Story*, Crown, 1988

Finler, Joel W, *The Hollywood Story* [the second revised edition], Wallflower Press, 2003

Fleming, Charles, *High Concept: Don Simpson And The Hollywood Culture Of Excess*, Doubleday, 1998

Gomery, Douglas, *The Hollywood Studio System*, St. Martin's Press, 1986

Hall, Phil, *The Encyclopedia Of Underground Movies: Films From The Fringes Of Cinema*, Michael Wiese Productions, 2004

Hayes, Dade & Bing, Jonathan, *Open Wide: How Hollywood Box Office Became A National Obsession*, Miramax Books, 2004

Henrie, Mark C, *Doomed Bourgeois In Love: Essays on the Films of Whit Stillman*, ISI Books, 2001

Hillier, Jim, *American Independent Cinema*, BFI, 1993

Hillier, Jim, *The New Hollywood*, Continuum, 1993

Hoberman, J & Rosenbaum, Jonathan, *Midnight Movies*, Harper and Row, 1983

Horsley, Jake, *Dogville vs. Hollywood*, Marion Boyars, 2005

Jackel, Anne, *European Film Industries*, BFI, 2003

Jancovich, Mark & Faire, Luc & Stubbings, Sarah, *The Place of the Audience: Cultural Geographies of Film Consumption*, BFI, 2003

King, Geoff, *American Independent Cinema*, Indiana University Press, 2005

King, Geoff, *New Hollywood Cinema: An Introduction*, Columbia University Press, 2002

Klinger, Barbara, *Beyond The Multiplex: Cinema, New Technologies, and The Home*, University of California Press, 2006

Kramer, Peter, *The New Hollywood From Bonnie and Clyde To Star Wars*, Wallflower Press, 2005

Levy, Emanuel, *Cinema Of Outsiders: The Rise of American Independent Film*, New York University Press, 1999

Lewis, Jon, *The End of Cinema As We Know It*, New York University Press, 2001

Lewis, Jon, *New American Cinema*, Duke University Press, 1998

Lipton, Lenny, *Independent Cinema*, Straight Arrow Books, 1972

Lyman, Rick, *Watching Movies*, Times Books, 2002

Lyons, Donald, *Independent Visions*, Ballantine Books, 1994

MacDonald, Scott, *A Critical Cinema 3: Interviews with Independent Filmmakers*, University of California Press, 1998

MacDonald, Scott, *A Critical Cinema 4: Interviews with Independent Filmmakers*, University of California Press, 2005

MacDonald, Scott, *A Critical Cinema 5: Interviews with Independent Filmmakers*, University of California Press, 2006

Mangold, James, *Cop Land and Heavy*, Faber and Faber, 1997

Mangold, James, *Girl, Interrupted*, Faber and Faber, 1999

Mangold, James, *Heavy*, Scenario, Volume 1, No. 3, Summer 1995

Mathijs, Ernest & Mendik, Xavier (eds), *Alternative Europe: Eurotrash And Exploitation Cinema Since 1945*, Wallflower Press, 2004

McDonagh, Maitland, *Filmmaking On The Fringe: The Good, The Bad, And The Deviant Directors*, Citadel Press, 1994

Mendik, Xavier & Harper, Graeme (eds), *Unruly Pleasures: The Cult Film And Its Critics*, Fab Press, 2000

Medik, Xavier & Schneider, Steven Jay, *Underground USA: Filmmaking Beyond The Hollywood Canon*, Wallflower Press, 2002

Merritt, Greg, *Celluloid Mavericks: A History of American Independent Film*, Thunder's Mouth, 2000

Miller, Toby & Govil, Nitin & McMurria, John & Maxwell, Richard & Wang, Ting, *Global Hollywood 2*, University of California Press, 2005

Morton, Jim & Rice, Boyd, *Incredibly Strange Films*, ReSearch issue No. 10, 1986

Mottram, James, *The Sundance Kids: How the Mavericks Took Back Hollywood*, Faber and Faber, 2006

Molyneaux, Gerry, *John Sayles: An Unauthorized Biography Of The Pioneering Indie Filmmaker*, Renaissance Books, 2000

Murphy, Robert, *The British Cinema Book*, Second Edition, BFI, 2001

Neale, Steve & Smith, Murray (eds), *Contemporary Hollywood Cinema*, Routledge, 1998

Pierson, John, *Spike, Mike, Slackers & Dykes: A Guided Tour Across a Decade of American Independent Cinema*, Miramax, 1995

Pribram, E Deirdre, *Cinema and Culture: Independent Film in the United States, 1980–2001*, Peter Lang, 2002

Robinson, Patrick, *Film Facts*, Billboard Books, 2001

Russell, Bertrand, *The Conquest Of Happiness*, Liveright, 1996 edition

Sayles, John, *Thinking in Pictures: The Making of the Movie Matewan*, Houghton Mifflin, 1987

Schaefer, Eric, *'Bold! Daring! Shocking! True': A History Of*

*Exploitation Films, 1919–1959*, Duke University Press, 1999

Shone, Tom, *Blockbuster: How Hollywood Learned To Stop Worrying And Love The Summer*, Free Press, 2004

Slide, Anthony, *The American Film Industry: A Historical Dictionary*, Limelight Editions, 1989

Smith, Gavin, *Sayles On Sayles*, Faber and Faber, 1998

Stillman, Whit, *Barcelona and Metropolitan: Tales of Two Cities*, Faber and Faber, 1994

Stillman, Whit, *The Last Days of Disco, With Cocktails at Petrossian Afterwards*, Farrar, Straus, Giroux, 2000

Sullivan, Monica (ed), *VideoHound's Independent Film Guide,* Visible Ink, 1997

Taylor, Thom, *The Big Deal: Hollywood's Million-Dollar Spec Script Market*, William Morrow, 1999

Waxman, Sharon, *Rebels on the Backlot: Six Maverick Directors and How They Conquered the Hollywood Studio System*, HarperCollins, 2005

Wilson, Michael & Rosenfelt, Deborah Silverton, *Salt of the Earth*, Feminist Press, 1978

Winter, Jessica, *The Rough Guide to American Independent Film,* Rough Guides, 2006

## Magazine articles

Anonymous, *The Economist*, 20 May 2006, p 88

Jensen, Jeff, 'David Lynch wants to get in your bloodstream', *Entertainment Weekly*, 8 December 2006, pp 40–43

## Websites and Podcasts

Helpful and entertaining interview podcasts can be found in The Creative Writing magazine at:
http://www.creativescreenwriting.com/podcasts/main.html

Chuck Tryon's blog entry of 10 October 2005, 'What is Independent Cinema', gives a good summary of the issues that surround definitions of the term, with good talkbacks from readers:
http://chutry.wordherders.net/archives/004970.html

Lisa Rosman's essay in her blog The Broad View offers an elegantly written account of her frustration with independent cinema, within the context of remarks about Zoe Cassavetes's *Broken English* (2007):
http://lisarosman.blogspot.com/

Insightful interviews with Jill Sprecher can be found at:
http://www.austinchronicle.com/gyrobase/Issue/story?oid=oid%3A96019
http://www.montrealserai.com/2002_Volume_15/15_4/Article_3.htm
http://www.filmfreakcentral.net/notes/jsprecherinterview.htm

The Cinetopia website can be found at:
http://www.cinetopiatheaters.com/

A clearing house for information about Whit Stillman can be found at:
http://www.whitstillman.org/

# INDEX

DVD contents

*Film as a Subversive Art: Amos Vogel and Cinema 16*

An hour-long filmed profile of Amos Vogel, 82-year old New York resident and Austrian emigré, founder of the New York Film Festival and America's most important film society, Cinema 16.

Edited version, produced and directed by Paul Cronin
© Sticking Place Films 2003
www.thestickingplace.com

The new edition of Amos Vogel's book *Film as a Subversive Art* (C.T. Edition, 2006) is available from all good book-sellers.